D1486167

RAPHAEL

MASTERS AND MOVEMENTS

LUCIANO BERTI

Translated from the Italian by SYLVIA SPRIGGE

RAPHAEL

W. W. NORTON & COMPANY INC.
NEW YORK

ND623
.R2
B463
cop. 2
0 01576495

© 1961 ISTITUTO ITALIANO D'ARTI GRAFICHE · BERGAMO · PRINTED IN ITALY
LIBRARY OF CONGRESS CATALOG CARD NUMBER 61-15340

The city of Urbino, where Raphael, the son of a fairly competent local painter, was born on April 6, 1483, was the capital of one of the smallest states in the political constellation which was Italy in the fifteenth century. As a centre of the arts and of the pursuit of culture, Urbino could certainly count as one of the choicest in the Renaissance.

Frederick, Duke of Montefeltro, who died the year before Raphael Sanzio's birth, was responsible for this. Away from home he had certainly been a professional *condottiere*, pursuing adventures with his men on behalf of third parties. While in the pay of Florence he was guilty of the ferocious sack of Volterra in 1472. Buts inside his hereditary realm it seems that he was an excellent and much loved prince, and undoubtedly a patron of the most rare taste.

Duke Frederick built the splendid Ducal Palace which still dominates the little hill town, the Palace which for Baldassare Castiglione was 'not a palace but to all appearances a city in the shape of a palace'. It was a masterpiece of formal beauties and technical perfection. According to Bernardino Baldi, writing in the fifteenth century, 'The open galleries, the halls and the rooms all have double vaulting and are built with such wonderful artifice that in the whole of this great edifice one cannot see a single wood or iron spike... Whence it may be observed how competent was the architect and how munificent the prince, and not only from this, but because of the way both of them had an eye to the eternal structure, and spared nought towards achieving it. Thus, there are no wooden ceilings in this palace, such as quickly darken, get the worm, and offer a thousands perils from fire... In the matter of light the architect was equally cunning, for in this great building there is not a room but is not most comfortably lit, and this is due to the excellent disposition of the courtyards and the apartments... Moreover the staircases throughout the palace are arranged with superb judgment, so that without using the principal ones, it is possible to go up and come down by many others which are very convenient... '

The main architecture was undertaken by the Dalmatian Luciano Laurana, who was then succeeded by the famous Sienese, Francesco di Giorgio Martini, called in to decorate the palace and to work for Duke Frederick's Urbino along with many other masters of the Renaissance in sculpture and painting, whose renown had spread all over Italy and whom the Duke had admired from the beginning.

We need only mention among the sculptors the Florentine, Maso di Bartolomeo, who designed the gateway of San Domenico, with its jewel-like lunette by Luca della Robbia; his fellow-citizens, Domenico Rosselli and Francesco di Simone Ferrucci, who worked with the more exuberant Lombard, Ambrogio Barocci, in the delicate ornamentation of the cornices, the doorways, the windows and the stuccos of the royal apartments, and another Dalmatian, Francesco Laurana, who made the portrait of the Duchess Battista Sforza — a noble and idealized bust which is in the Bargello Museum in Florence today.

Duke Frederick of Montefeltro was fortunate indeed in his painter, Piero della Francesca, discovering in him an exceptional artist who was able to create a special, aesthetic atmosphere in Urbino. Under his influence came other artists, for example the two Lauranas, the architect and the sculptor. Piero's works at Urbino are the little but the exquisite *Flagellation*, now in the museum of the Palace, with its crystalline perspective and its light which bears comparison with the purest daylight; the portraits of the Duke himself and of his Duchess which now hang in the Uffizi, both painted in profile, most composed and solemn, presiding over the ample panorama of their lands in the background; the altarpiece which now hangs in the Brera, but was once in the church of San Bernardino in Urbino whose architecture, contemporary with the figures, caught from them some of their solemn monumental spirit. Bramante, born in this district, learnt much from that church, we know, and certainly found it helpful in his architectural development.

Paolo Uccello worked in Urbino also. He left a delicious fable on a predella there. The Flemish artist Justin of Ghent and the Spaniard Pedro Berruguete painted a series of portraits of famous men for Duke Frederick's study, as well as other works. Melozzo da Forlì painted Frederick's son, Guidobaldo. Botticelli made drawings for the intarsia work on the Palace portals, and possibly also for those amazing and most beautiful of all intarsias, in the Duke's study, which Baccio Pontelli executed, inventing the illusion of open cupboards and landscapes full of musical instruments, arms, books and sculptures.

There was, too, the great library which the Duke built and used, spending some 30,000 ducats on it; the tapestries, the silver and the furniture which once graced the ducal dwelling; the very beauty of the whole architecture from the little turrets high up on the walls overlooking the countryside to the wide high expanse of the façade on the piazza; the final courtyard, gathered as it were into its own peaceful and serene movement; the vast halls and the hanging gardens. All this was to provide the setting in which, later on in 1506, Castiglione placed the conversations of his *Courtier*. Here, meanwhile, we may picture Giovanni Santi hand in hand with his shy and much admired son, who was so well disposed towards the arts.

In thus recapturing the feeling of fifteenth-century Urbino we do no more than every traditional biographer of Raphael has done, but we do take note of a possible objection: is this scene really requisite as a preface to the art of Raphael?

The relation between the artist and his birthplace which an author normally tries to establish, frequently appears as logically quite undemonstrable. Thereupon a search in depth is undertaken — ancestral or psychological factors are considered, or merely romantic suggestions. Let us consider three Masters of the Cinquecento, among whom Raphael. Of what account is Caprera, the birthplace of Michelangelo, in that artist's life, seeing that his father happened to be the mayor of that place for that year and that Michelangelo was taken away from Caprera when just under a month old, never to return? And what about the more cheerful but equally modest village of Vinci, in the case of Leonardo? And was it absolutely necessary for Raphael to be born in Urbino, and not, for instance in Città di Castello, where he actually began his career as an Umbrian follower of Perugino?

But there remains what Michelangelo (who was given in charge of a wet nurse at Settignano, the wife of one of the many stone cutters there) said later to Vasari, if only in fun: ' Giorgio, if I have nothing of much value in my talents, that comes of being born in the subtle air of your Arezzo district; but with the milk I drew from my wet-nurse I drew the chisel and the mallet with which I make figures '.

One might prolong the rhetoric by saying that to be born on the bare plateau of la Verna, astride the sources of the Arno and the Tiber, Michelangelo was destined to spend his working life in those two cities which lie on the banks of those two rivers; that his art has an analogy with the virile and titanic character of the mountain; that Michelangelo, rather than use the canvas or the wall on which to paint illusions, preferred a substance more plastically real and more massive in body with which to make his architectonic limbs, or to attack the marble with his furious chisel, in order to discover the suffering heroic figures imprisoned there.

Leonardo, offspring of the love of a young notary for one of his peasant girls, was, on the other hand, born and bred at Vinci on the southern slopes of Monte Albano, in a gentle countryside full of vines and olive groves. That is the setting of his earliest imagined memory of a kite which flew at his cradle and pecked him several times on the lips, which Freud interpreted as a mark of homosexual tendencies. At Vinci were the images of his grandmother, of a very young stepmother wedded by the notary immediately after his birth, of his mother who had also married and lived in a nearby village still on the master's land, and all these images embedded themselves in his subconscious until one day he would create the duplicated maternal sweetness of his *Madonna and St Anne with the Holy Child*. Leonardo, a ' natural ' child, growing up in the heart of the countryside, would always and above all love nature, even when he has

PLATE I - ANGEL (1500-1501). (FRAGMENT OF THE ALTARPIECE OF S. NICOLA DA TOLEN-
TINO) - BRESCIA, CIVIC MUSEUM ▶

PLATE 3 - ANNUNCIATION (1502-1503) - VATICAN GALLERY

◀ PLATE 2 - ST SEBASTIAN (C. 1503) - BERGAMO, CARRARA ACADEMY

PLATE 4 - PRESENTATION IN THE TEMPLE (1502-1503) - VATICAN, GALLERY

developed his terrible and universal genius. Nature would be the chief object of his enquiry as a scientist, of his contemplation as an artist.

Raphael was born in Urbino in the house of a painter. The house is there today with its plain brick front, even with its supporting arches; the doors and windows have Renaissance forms. On the ground floor Giovanni Santi painted and gilded; on the first floor there are three rooms in one of which Raphael was born. Giovanni had received Piero della Francesca in this house in 1469, on one of the latter's visits to Urbino.

Raphael was his mother's only son. She was Battista Ciarla's daughter, a shopkeeper. Her name was Magia, and she brought with her a modest dowry of 150 florins. She died in 1491 when her boy was eight. Giovanni then wed a young woman called Bernadina. When he died in 1494, she was expecting a child who was named Elizabeth. He left her a fair legacy of 860 florins. Arguments arose between the widow and the paternal uncle and tutor of Raphael, the archdeacon Don Bartolomeo. One of Raphael's paternal aunts was Santa, the wife of a tailor, who also lived on in Giovanni's house and looked after the child with the stepmother. Another was Margherita, whose son, Girolamo Vagnini, was to insist, together with others, that an epitaph should be inscribed in the Pantheon in Rome (where Raphael is buried) to Maria Francesca Bibbiena, niece of the famous Cardinal of the same name, who had been affianced to Raphael. But Raphael was especially devoted to an uncle on his mother's side, Simone Ciarla, to whom he sent a letter in 1508 which we here reproduce at length, as a very clear indication of his attitude to the family and his state, and full of human interest and an artist's practical concerns.

' To my dear Uncle Simone di Battista di Ciarla in Urbino.

Dear to me as father,
I received your letter in which I learned of the death of our Illustrious Duke [Guidobaldo], on whom may God have mercy, and of course I could not read your letter without tears, but let that

pass: one must accept what cannot be remedied and submit to the will of God. The other day I wrote to my uncle the priest asking him to send me the panel of Our Lady which belongs to the prefect's wife [Giovanna Feltria, Guidobaldo's sister and wife of Giovanni della Rovere, the prefect of Rome]. He did not send it, and I bid you to remind him of it the next time someone is travelling, so that I can satisfy the lady. Also, dearest uncle, please tell the priest and Santa too that should Taddeo Taddei [a client and close friend of Raphael's] the Florentine about whom we have often spoken come their way, they should make him very welcome without any stint whatever, and you also be very dear to him because of my love, for I am as much beholden to him as to any man alive. And about that panel [possibly the Madonna of the Baldacchino], I did not suggest a price, nor will I if I can, for it is best that it should be rewarded according to its merit. That is why I haven't written and still cannot advise you. But according to what the patron of that panel said to me, I shall have work here and in France for about 300 ducats in gold; after the holiday perhaps I shall write to tell you what I get for the panel: I have made the drawing and I will write after Easter. Further, I would like to have an introduction to the Gonfaloniere of Florence from the Prefect [Della Rovere] and a few days ago I wrote to uncle and to Giovanni of Rome [the Gian Cristofero Romano, who was busy as a sculptor at that time in Urbino?] to ask for it: it would certainly help me a lot in connexion with a hall which is to be frescoed [the Hall of Palazzo Vecchio where Raphael hoped to succeed Leonardo, when the latter left for Rome?] which is in the gift of the Prefect. I do ask you, if you can, to send it to me because I think that any request about me to the Prefect will be met, and recommend me to him a thousand times as one of his old servants and familiars. Nothing more. Remember me to the Master... to Rodolfo and to all the others. April 21. 1508.

Your

Raffaello, dipintore in Fiorenza '

Now, having outlined the domestic setting in which Raphael worked, what influence can we say that Urbino had upon his art?

Certainly no precise stylistic influences. He has been linked in some way with the simplified and serene classic art of the Della Robbias, but that is not to say that he caught this from the single lunette at San Domenico, rather than elsewhere and later through Perugino (who himself demonstrably owed much to the Della Robbia patterns), or directly during his stay in Florence. Raphael's sense of most ample spaciousness cannot either be directly associated with Piero della Francesca, in whose work space is always created by virtue of perspectives within a cubic and geometric framework which is obvious even when concealed, and has been analysed to the utmost limit of the vision. Raphael's landscapes, on the contrary, quickly merge into the indefinite and are mere positions in the infinite cosmic sphere, thereby sharing in the lovely secret which Perugino discovered in his own Umbrian painting.

Nor is it certain that Raphael drew on other Urbino figurative arts for his style, for they all belong to previous generations aesthetically, to the pre-Renaissance fifteenth century during which linear surface values and the analytic method had prevailed, whereas Raphael and the sixteenth century are concerned with volume and synthesis.

Any paternal influence on Raphael has long been denied — we called his father a fairly competent painter, but we must add that he was eclectic, mediocre, provincial and somewhat wooden. Recent critics have moreover rejected as nonexistent, or practically so, another influence once held to be important, that of Timoteo Viti of Urbino, who returned home from the French School in 1495, when Raphael was probably just entering the circle of Perugino. Nor can Evangelista di Pian di Meleto be called an influence. He was a pupil of Giovanni Santi and the first fellow artist of the young Raphael.

Since Raphael's artistic experiences occurred quickly outside his native state, and taking into account his receptive genius for absorbing other fundamental experiences and his own creative capacity, we must of necessity discount stylistic influences of Urbino on him.

But on a wider plane it is possible that Urbino counted for something in the art of its great son.

Let us consider the particular nature of the city's artistic atmosphere. It did not arise out of a collective vitality as happened in Florence, where the figure arts flowered already in the late thirteenth century among an economically rising bourgeoisie which had exceptional political strength. That bourgeoisie's developed ideology — in other words, realism —, its scientific rationalism, its noted secularism, moral austerity and measured individualism (as Antal says) informed the creations of its artists. The art of Florence was born of this social stock and always manifested these origins. From Giotto to Masaccio, from Donatello and Masaccio to Michelangelo, Florentine art always appears realistic and logical, sober and synthetic, permeated by human and moral values. Leonardo is a lyricist of the sweetest kind, but also and continually an inexorable scientist. Michelangelo reflects the politico-religious crisis of Savonarola; his statue of David is a symbol of democratic forces and of bodily and spiritual values common to all men, and Michelangelo feels the call to take part in the final defensive struggle of the Florentine Republic. But the Palace in Urbino was the creation of a prince, of a solitary hero. It had been built not by calling together local artistic energies, but by summoning various foreign masters. It rises like a colossus, isolated from the modest city with its rather rustic houses and steep little alleys: a fortress, royal residence, museum, library, all forming a complete and self-sufficient citadel, a social and intellectual acropolis. And in Raphael's sight it must have represented a fundamental archetype. In Rome he would become the artist of the supreme synthesis of the Papal Court. His vision of man would become ever more aristocratically classifying and his concern would be not so much with science, as was the case in Florence, but with form, with that very form which Piero della Francesca had created in an idealized and sublimated version, as the aesthetic style of the court of Duke Frederick of Montefeltro.

One knows the rich variety of the ornamentation inside the Ducal Palace. Raphael's characteristic lies precisely in that 'univer-

PLATE 6 - THE THREE GRACES (C. 1504) - CHANTILLY, CONDÉ MUSEUM

PLATE 7 - CONNESTABILE MADONNA - LENINGRAD, HERMITAGE

PLATE 8 - MADONNA DEL GRANDUCA (C. 1505) - FLORENCE, PITTI GALLERY

SELF-PORTRAIT (?) (C. 1504) - OXFORD, ASHMOLEAN ▶

STUDY FOR THE PRESENTATION IN THE TEMPLE (1502-1503) - OXFORD, ASHMOLEAN

MADONNA OF THE POMEGRANATE (C. 1504) - VIENNA, ALBERTINA ▶

STUDY FOR ST GEORGE AND THE DRAGON (C. 1504-1505) - FLORENCE, UFFIZI

sality' which Vasari found in his art. In fact the chief object in his art will not be only the human body (that is, man) as with Michelangelo, but he will also be the painter of landscape, of history, the expert in archaeology, qualified in every kind of decorative pattern, in tapestry, in stuccos, in grotesques.

Moreover, the Palace of Urbino is not contained in a theoretical, prescribed form like the palaces in Florence; it spreads according to the terrain and the accidents of its hillside with something of the spirit of contemporary organic architecture. Around it and around the city lie the wide and solitary hillsides of the Marches. Likewise with Raphael we shall often find that the centre of civilisation or aristocracy or humanity in his composition is immersed in a deep breath of nature, for instance in the *Sposalizio* at the Brera (PL. 5), and in the landscape backgrounds in the two *Portraits of Maddalena and Angelo Doni* in the Pitti (PL. 13 and PL. 12), and in the background of the *Dispute over the Holy Sacrament*, in the Vatican (page 53).

This was how Urbino left its mark in the art of Raphael. And it may be that just as Castiglione chose that Palace and that Court as the scene of converse about his perfect Courtier, so the son of this city may represent, above all others, the perfect artist of the Cinquecento.

By October 1, 1504 the prefect's wife, Giovanna Felicia Feltria Rovere, of whom we read in Raphael's letter of 1508, had already written from Urbino to the Gonfaloniere of the Florentine Republic, Piero Soderini, to introduce and recommend the twenty-one year old Raphael: ' The bearer of this letter is Raphael, painter of Urbino, who has a fine skill in his work and has decided on a considerable stay in Florence, in order to learn more. And because his father was gifted and I liked him much, and the son is modest and a kind youth, I love him dearly and would wish him to become really accomplished, I recommend him earnestly to your Lordship...'

What had the 'modest and kind youth' 'with a fine skill in his work' been doing in the years before, having now decided to go to Florence, with the desire to perfect himself there? (And indeed, as we shall see, only in that city could he find the wherewithal to become the Raphael that history knows).

Apart from a few well-documented works, art history has had to be content with guesswork and rare dates in this period before the autumn of 1504, so that opinions are liable to vary about it. The view once held that Timoteo Viti was a formative influence long before that of Perugino, is giving ground to another view held by Professor Longhi.

According to this view Raphael was in touch with Perugino in the last decade of the Quattrocento, as an adolescent, very soon after the death of his father, and Longhi accordingly attributes certain ' minor ' works to that period — not *The Young Warrior's Dream* in London and *The Three Graces* at Chantilly (PL. 6), which had hitherto been attributed to Raphael when little more than a boy painter, although they are fairly accomplished. The painter's beginnings are, in fact, deemed to be less brilliant, but by contrast, more likely.

One of the works which would thus qualify is the fresco of the *Madonna and Child* in Raphael's house at Urbino, which Cavalcaselle attributed to Giovanni Santi and romantically suggested might be the figure of Magia with her little son Raphael, asleep on her knee. Both Professors Ragghianti and Longhi attribute it to Raphael, as tradition indeed had it. Longhi further compares the profile of the Virgin, very precise and slightly grimacing, with that of the woman who holds the new born Madonna in the Predella of Perugino (1497) in Santa Maria Novella at Fano, in which therefore Raphael is supposed to have collaborated.

Actually the babe in the fresco in Urbino is softer in construction than the usually rather hard lines of Giovanni Santi, while the Madonna's profile with the veiled cap over the pad seems closer to the *Portrait of the Duchess Battista Sforza* by Piero della Francesca, now in the Uffizi; likewise the curious iconography of the mother intent on a book on the lectern might have been inspired by the *Portrait of the Duke Frederick of Montefeltro* by Pedro Beruguete, regally concentrated in reading, now in the Ducal Palace. Is this fresco then the work of Raphael at the end of the fifteenth century, linked in imagination with remembered works in his native city, but already under the influence of Perugino? In the latter, by the way, one has noted a singular renewal of vigour towards 1495, like a dip in a *fons juventutis*, which might correspond with the arrival of Raphael in his school.

Along the lines of this hypothesis, then, Raphael is often with Perugino not only in Perugia but also in Florence in journeys home and to the Adriatic (Perugino was at this time indeed commissioned for work in Fano and in Sinigallia), and he stays a while at the foot of the pass at Città di Castello (where in fact Raphael was to have work on hand) and in nearby San Sepolcro, where Longhi attributes a banner to Raphael, which hangs in the Picture Gallery of Città di Castello. The face on the Crucifixion is Peruginesque, but the Madonna of Mercy on the other side roughly imitates this famous subject in Piero della Francesca's Polyptych at Borgo San Sepolcro.

Certainly the banner is somewhat tart, but to sustain the attribution there is the soft yet square symbolism of the figures which well conforms to the hand of Giovanni Santi's son rather than to a later follower of Perugino.

We would go further, having got thus far, and suggest that this is a Raphael who has been to Florence, in other words that the Madonna in the house at Urbino who seems to sit in profile against a cushion, on a simple square seat with the child oblivious in her lap, reminds us in all these particular details of the *Madonna of the Staircase* which the very young Michelangelo had already carved in Florence, and which, even though Michelangelo was away in Rome, a young foreigner, desirous of learning, might have managed to see.

However, one has to recall the letter of 1504 of Giovanna Della Rovere presenting Raphael ' who has decided on a considerable stay in Florence in order to learn more '. Clearly, supposing he had already visited the city, he could not have stayed long or have made himself known to many people.

In such a brief study we may not enter into learned discussions. Nor shall we dwell on the debate as to Raphael's assistance to Perugino (for example in the frescoes in the Cambio in Perugia). Let us consider straightaway what is known for certain about him, and therefore turn to the first year of the new century.

On December 10, 1500, the seventeen year old son of Giovanni Santi together with Evangelista di Pian di Meleto — who besides being a disciple of Giovanni Santi was also his executor and thereby in some sense Raphael's guardian — were commissioned to paint a large altar-piece of the *Beatification of Nicola da Tolentino* for the church of Sant'Agostino in Città di Castello. Such an order shows that Raphael must already have already won favour in that city: there is a banner in its museum today with the *Creation of Eve* on one side and the *Trinity with Sebastian and Roch* on the other painted by Raphael, which was supposed to belong to 1499 or a little after, having been ordered as an *ex-voto* by the city for the plague which broke out that year. Today some critics date it slightly later.

The Sant'Agostino altar-piece was finished in 1501. In an earthquake in 1789 it was completely destroyed, but some preparatory drawings are known in the Museum at Lille and Oxford, and a partial eighteenth-century copy exists in the Museum at Città di Castello, and a fragment in the Naples Museum of *God the Father* and the *Virgin*, from the upper part of the altar-piece, held to be by Evangelista, and another fragment from the right hand, the *Half figure of an angel* in the Museum at Brescia, certainly by Raphael.

The *Angel* (PL. I) is clearly of Peruginesque pattern, but it also enjoys a more youthful freshness which is ingenuous, chaste but bold, concealed behind its splendid and full beauty. In the general design now in Lille (where God the Father at the top is substituted by an ordinary personage and the saint is drawn in the nude), two Perugino motifs are merged together: *i.e.* the position of the figures over an arch which opens on the landscape in the background (hardly discernible in the drawing but clearly visible in the Città di Castello copy); and the division of the composition into two parts, one attached to the earth and the other with the figures in the air. These latter figures however are all three half figures (and not, as was usual in Perugino's time, whole figures inevitably kneeling or seated). In this way a certain fifteenth-century fidelity to nature is simplified without being offended. Then the very central position (among all those present) of the devil on the pedestal, just struck to earth, is original, as is the figure of the saint, who has a thoughtful and humble face despite his moment of triumph (in the Lille drawing). In fact Raphael from now on displays his inventiveness in composition assuredly, but with a profound newness.

From this second Lille drawing we may consider an influence of Pinturicchio which Longhi dates between 1501-02 and to which Vasari had referred when he wrote that Raphael assisted in making the drawings for the famous series of frescoes in the Library of the Cathedral of Siena which Pinturicchio began in 1502. On the back of this drawing at the top, several swans are sketched, one of them pecking at a snake, not unlike those which embellish the little Kinnaird *Resurrection* in the Sao Paolo Museum in Brazil, a work which must be attributed to Raphael according to drawings at Oxford, and whose ornate and decorative manner betray Pinturicchio's influence.

But in the Mond *Crucifixion* in the National Gallery in London which was painted for San Domenico in Città di Castello and dated, it seems, 1503, the contemplative severity after the manner of Perugino is again evident. In the predella (Lisbon Museum; from the Cook Collection, Richmond) of *Jerome raising a man from the dead* the story is told in a pretty fusion of the two styles, a style freer and more modern than the Umbrian painters usually practised.

When compared with the St John in the Mond *Crucifixion* and with the landscape behind him, the *Bust of Sebastian* in the Carrara Academy at Bergamo (PL. 2) seems to be of the same period. Here the robe is richly embroidered and at first the figure seems serenely sentimental, but in reality it is too full of stress and too communicative (the martyr's arrow sticks out from the hand towards the viewer in perspective; the womanly and melancholy face of the saint is caught in a slight inclination of the head).

Also during this period Raphael must have painted the *Solly Madonna* and the *Madonna with Jerome and Francis*, both in the Berlin Museum, and both first attempts at subjects which were to become a speciality of his.

Meanwhile in about 1502-03 Raphael was painting the *Coronation of the Virgin* for the chapel of Maddalena degli Oddi in the church of St Francis in Perugia which has found its way to the Vatican Museum, and was, together with its predella, transferred to canvas and removed to safety at the time of Napoleon's invasion of Italy. This painting has the archaic Della Robbia 'partition on two levels', but it also has two semicircles of apostles and angels superimposed, such as clearly mark the attempt to pass from a flat geometry to a spherical treatment of space. One never finds this in Perugino. One day it was to turn into the grandiose conception of the *Dispute over the Holy Sacrament* (pag. 53).

In the *Annunciation* of the Predella (PL. 3) the two protagonists meet under a vast portico, wide and rounded as in a Perugino scene: one should compare this with the Perugino *Annunciation* in Fano and see how Raphael now paints columns instead of the flat Fano pilasters, and how one's eye can travel freely in the ample area between the two figures out towards the clear blues of the background. And again in the Vatican predella, in the *Presentation of the Holy Child* (PL. 4) the whole architecture breathes more freely against the sky on both sides, than in the same scene in Fano.

And then at last in the *Sposalizio* at the Brera (PL. 5) originally painted for the Albizzini family, for the chapel of St Joseph in the church of St Francis in Città di Castello, boldly signed and dated upon the arch of the entrance to the temple RAPHAEL URBINAS MDIIII, a similar painting by Perugino is far surpassed, and here, outside Florence, one of the basic documents of Italian classic painting is created.

Perugino's *Sposalizio* was finished in Caen but had arrived in Perugia. It had an horizontal line of figures in the forefront with the priest in the centre, and the groom and bride on either side, with an octagonal temple in the background with three doors, one facing the viewer on the same axis as the priest, and the other two seen in profile. In fact it conformed to a perfect but mechanical and symmetrical arrangement of fundamentally flat figures. In the Brera *Sposalizio*, on the other hand, the central scene of this not very big altar-piece is firmly planted and not relegated high up as at Caen, and the temple tends towards the circular with its many-sided façades, doubtless under the influence of the new architecture of the Urbino artist Bramante and of his recently finished (1502) *Tempietto* in the courtyard of San Pietro in Montorio in Rome. Moreover the little group of figures in the foreground, almost too modest, is disposed in a slightly convex manner which echoes the curve of the building and so tends to make a curve round the centre-piece of the painting. The temple is the dominating feature of the work. The eye is drawn to it beyond the sacred scene following the rhythm of the pavement designed in strips and squares. The temple seems to gather within itself, in a spherical and centralized way, all the immensity of the surrounding area. And what is religion if not a similar search for a spiritual centre?

Here Raphael's imagination was superb. It must have owed much to the civilisation of Urbino where Piero della Francesca's geometric idealisation held sway (compare Piero's portrait of *Frederick of Montefeltro* in the Uffizi with the bust of the Duke set like a large tower watching over his lands in the background: whoever is the Pieresque author of *Architectural View* in the Palace at Urbino, it too is centred round a circular temple), but much also to Perugino, to whom Raphael owed that sense of immense space which lucid skies give, as well the feeling for a sweet contemplation and an almost melancholy mysticism. This great work may well close the first period of Raphael's achievements.

In Florence in that first autumn of 1504 and until he returned for a time to Perugia the following year, Raphael must have had a good look at the so much vaster and more various assortment of figurative arts, out in the open and in the making, than he could ever have seen in his birthplace, even in the times of his good father, in the Umbrian province where he started his painter's career.

Florence at that time signified not only the vision and the direct study of a whole previous century of the Renaissance, which had proved a revelation and an inspiration for the rest of Italy, but also a kind of city-museum uncommonly rich in collections of antiquities and of foreign works. Just to live there was to experience daily this new and astonishing maturity, occurring so naturally and developing such perfection.

Leonardo, back from Milan, was working at his *Gioconda* and his *St Anne*. Michelangelo had just finished his giant *David* and was finishing his *Doni tondo*; both were about to compete inside the Palazzo Vecchio for the Battle frescoes of the *Anghiari* and of *Cascina*. And they were not two lonely stars in a void. Lorenzo di Credi, Piero di Cosimo, Fra Bartolomeo and Mariotto Albertinelli and even Perugino, a frequent visitor, were all active in Florence — lesser but most lively talents who paved the way into the new century along the lower roads, especially with the severe, classical and simplified morality of Fra Bartolomeo, the deep rich technical ability of Lorenzo di Credi, amply open to Flemish influences, and Piero di Cosimo's humorous vein and northern fantasies.

To this first Florentine moment in Raphael's life probably belong a little bunch of extremely minutely executed works, almost as though he were hesitant and anxious not to cut a bad figure in the new surroundings. They evidence a curiously insatiable knowledge, as of a man who does not yet know his way about a market and makes little odd purchases only. These considerations lead one to believe these might be very youthful works from Urbino days, but on closer examination the analysis seems to reveal a not striking but yet a ' classical ' character which could be explained by his having already tasted the air of Florence (Longhi).

Vasari writes: ' That most excellent painter studied the old frescoes of Masaccio in Florence, and what he saw of the works of Leonardo and Michelangelo made him study the more and thereby acquire extraordinary improvement in the art and in his style. While

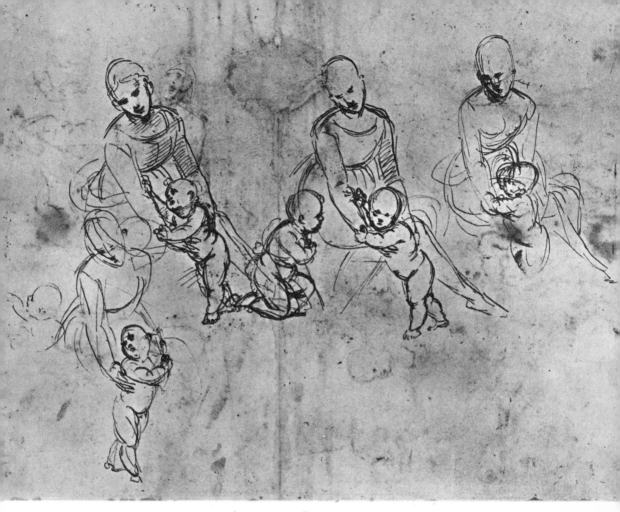

STUDY FOR A MADONNA (C. 1505-1506) - VIENNA, ALBERTINA

HEAD OF ST PLACIDO - OXFORD, ASHMOLEAN

PORTRAIT OF A YOUNG GIRL (C. 1505) - LONDON, BRITISH MUSEUM ▶

Raphael stayed in Florence he was closely associated with Fra Bartolomeo whom he liked much and whose colouring he often tried to imitate, and the encounter was the occasion of his teaching the good monk the skills of perspective to which the monk had, heretofore, not paid any attention '.

If we want to recapture the figure of this amazing young foreigner perfecting his art, rather than the famous but doubtful *Self-Portrait* in the Uffizi, we should not lightly cast aside the *Portrait* at Munich, attributed again recently by Volpe to Raphael. It comes from Florence where Hugford bought it in the eighteenth century from a private owner and Mengs then attributed it to Raphael. On the gold buttons of the jacket there is the name Raphael, but it is not clear whether this refers to the subject of the portrait or to the painter. The man there portrayed rather resembles, even to the 'ball nose', a *Portrait* at Hampton Court which has the same kind of inscription and which used to be considered a self-portrait by Raphael. Later it was not so considered and now again it is so claimed by Volpe. Both these portraits can stand fairly well alongside the portrait of Raphael given in Vasari's *Lives*, less well alongside the acknowledged self-portrait next to Sodoma, which Raphael painted in his *School of Athens.*

Nevertheless there are other supporting factors: the figure's position between two columns (a detail of Flemish origin), while beyond their base the countryside opens; moreover the iconography is similar to that of the *feminine figure* (PL. II) in the Borghese Gallery and to the study for a portrait in a Louvre drawing (page 36): indeed the latter, clearly inspired by the *Gioconda*, has much the same spirit as the portrait in Munich, of a frank and vivid effigy not overburdened by nobility.

As to the background of little trees sparkling with light one might in passing recall a painting by Memling now in Munich: in any case other Memlings were to be seen in Florence, such as the *Portrait of a Man with Landscape* painted in 1487, in the Uffizi, himself between two columns, or the *St Benedict* there, or the Corsini portrait. Imitations of Flemish details were very fashionable then in Filippino

Lippi's late work, right down to Lorenzo di Credi. But the portrait in Munich has much original invention and profound simplicity in the way the wood goes right up to the horizon by gradual steps in a great curve, itself inverse in direction and size to the short curve of the arm. The arm itself is bent and reveals the hand not in the foreground, as is usual with Memling, but withdrawn to hold up the cloak as in Michelangelo's *David*, which had only recently been erected in the Piazza della Signoria, where he likewise grips the terrible sling on his shoulder. It is, if we are not mistaken, an unusual pose.

In the *Young Warrior's Dream* in London, so familiar to our grammar schools students as ' Raphael's first work ', the perfect equilibrium in the composition of the two female figures in relation to the central tree which stands like the central rod of a pair of scales, might bring to mind the altar-piece of *Nicholas of Tolentino*, but its skill is more free and natural. In the other little panel of like origin and size (17 cm × 17 cm) and therefore probably related to the *Dream*, the Chantilly *Three Graces* (PL. 6) has such a soft relationship between the three nudes (inspired, it is believed, by a classic group in the Piccolomini Library in Siena Cathedral and by a medal made by Niccolò di Forzore Spinelli for Giovanna Albizzi-Tornabuoni) and such a mature and harmonious profundity, that it cannot be considered early work.

Salvini's comment is valid: ' The perfect harmony of the line movements and the modulations in the volume; the continuous bow-like movement of the outlines secretly corresponding with the modulated roundness of the bodies; the wide fullness of the curves outward, which prolong the broad extensive rhythm of the arms, made more noticeable by the slow knell of the three heads, dilate in the open space with a musical rhythm which re-echoes in the bend of the river and in the distant profile of the hills ''.

Similarly in the *Connestabile* Madonna in Leningrad (PL. 7) a pool of water also reflects the circular harmony of the round painting as does the simple inclination of the Virgin's head. It is the turn of the child's head, as graceful as the movements of the Three Graces, and reminding one of the *Terranuova* Madonna in Berlin, which fixes the date of the painting as not later than 1504. This latter Madonna indeed we would ascribe to the Florence period under Leonardo's influence: a kind of Virgin of the Rocks on the left but seen in perspective, and a movement as in the cartoon for St Anne, in the action of the child towards the infant Baptist. One notes the thin and bare small trees climbing up on the left (inspired perhaps by the *Tribute Money* fresco of Masaccio in the Carmine?) which lead up to the horizon of hills. They lie under a pale serene winter sky, and, up in the right hand corner become covered in snow — an unusual notation in Italian art.

In the *St Michael crushing Satan* and the *St George* in the Louvre, it may be that the inspiration comes from the drawings of Michelangelo and Leonardo for the Battle frescoes in Palazzo Vecchio, already famous by that time, for in the former (apart from the Boschlike fantasies of monsters, ghosts and a burning castle) Michael descends in a whirl on to Satan like one of the soldiers in Michelangelo's *Battle at Cascina*; and even the *St George* clearly owes much to Leonardo, especially to the *Battle of Anghiari*, in the dynamic swoop of the animals and the rider. This is clear also from the preparatory drawing in the Uffizi (page 24). In the painting however, the diagonal composition is perfectly balanced by the distant rising figure of the princess, and the serene depth of the space beyond the contestants brings with it a kind of gentle fairy tale quality rather than a dramatic clash of vital energies, such as there is in Leonardo's model.

Raphael's stay in Florence belongs to the period between the end of 1504 and most of 1508, with intervening return visits to Perugia and Urbino. In those four years we find a concentrated output comparable only with that of the later Mannerists in the sixteenth century. But Raphael's work has nothing to do with their eclectic and serial repetitions, nor with the fluid and continual experiments in mere formality of our modern art. His are solid masterpieces, each one demanding a serious invention in composition and a most strenuous perfection in carrying out the invention. Nor may one forget that almost from the first moment of his sojourn in Florence Raphael's art came to such sudden maturity as to compete with that of Leonardo and of Michelangelo.

Let us look at the list of works. Besides the first Florentine essays to which we have just referred, the small *Colonna Altar-piece* is believed to have been made at the end of 1504, early 1505. Its predella is partly in the Metropolitan, partly in the National Gallery and in part in the Gardner Museum in Boston. It was painted for the sisters of Saint Anthony in Perugia and begun before Raphael went to Florence, and probably finished after he left. Then there is the *Granduca Madonna* in the Pitti in Florence, and the *Cowper Madonna* in the National Gallery of Washington, which has the effigy of the church of St Bernadino at Urbino in the background (but we are not certain about this) and might tally with the Madonna painted for the Prefect's wife, Giovanna Feltria, mentioned in the letter we quoted of 1508.

The *Ansidei Madonna* in London bears the date 1506. It bears the name of the family in Perugia for which it was painted and may have been begun before the visit to Florence. The critics date the *Holy Family with Saint Joseph* in Leningrad and the *Portrait of a young woman* in the Borghese Gallery in Rome between 1505-06. The *Vierge de la Maison d'Orléans* at Chantilly belongs to 1506, like the *Christ blessing* at Brescia; the Washington *Saint George and the Dragon* was painted as a present for the King of England from Duke Guidobaldo of Urbino, who had received the Order of the Garter in 1506. The *Madonna of the Goldfinch* at the Uffizi, the *Portraits of Maddalena and Angelo Doni* at the Pitti, and the *Donna Gravida* also there, all belong to this period. And the *Madonna im Gruenen* at Vienna is dated 1506.

The following paintings belong round about 1507: the *Deposition* in the Borghese Gallery (dated) which was made for the chapel of Atalanta Baglioni in San Francesco al Prato, Perugia; the *Madonna Carnigiani* in Munich, the *Madonna dell'Agnello* in Madrid also dated (it seems) 1507; the *Bridgewater Madonna* in the Ellesmere Collection in London and the *Holy Family under Palm* there, the *St Cathe-*

PLATE 9 - MADONNA DEL CARDELLINO (C. 1506) - FLORENCE, PITTI GALLERY

PLATE 10 - SELF-PORTRAIT (C. 1504-1505) - MUNICH, ALTE PINAKOTHEK

PLATE 11 - PORTRAIT OF A YOUNG WOMAN (C. 1505-1506) - ROME, BORGHESE GALLERY ▶

PLATE 12 - PORTRAIT OF ANGELO DONI (C. 1506) - FLORENCE, PITTI GALLERY

44

PLATE 13 - PORTRAIT OF MADDALENA DONI (C. 1506) - FLORENCE, PITTI GALLERY

PLATE 14 - DEPOSITION (1507) - ROME, BORGHESE GALLERY

PLATE 15 - DISPUTE OVER THE HOLY SACRAMENT (C. 1509). DETAIL - VATICAN
STANZA OF THE SEGNATURA

rine in the National Gallery and the *Belle Jardinière* at the Louvre, which is dated 1507.

Then there is *La Muta* painted in Florence and formerly hung in the Uffizi, but transferred in 1927 by order of Mussolini to the Ducal Palace at Urbino, a transfer subsequently confirmed by the Italian Republic. But it does not properly belong there, being clearly a portrait of an unknown Florentine lady and in the Florentine tradition, and only goes to show the blatant lack of historical sense on the part of a ruler pandering to provincial feelings. Far better had the melancholy Duke Guidobaldo (he was impotent and ill) and his comely wife Elisabetta Gonzaga, so highly praised by Castiglione, been sent to their own city, instead of still hanging in the Uffizi, where they are attributed to Raphael. They certainly came from Urbino as part of the well-documented legacy of Urbino to the Medici in 1631.

Lastly the following also belong to the period around 1508: the *Tempi Madonna* in Munich, the *Madonna del Baldacchino* at the Pitti, which was begun a few years earlier for the Dei family and intended to be placed in the Florentine church of Santo Spirito, but was left unfinished after Raphael left for Rome; the *Esterhazy Madonna* in Budapest which was perhaps begun in Florence but finished in Rome, as can be seen from the landscape with Roman ruins in the background; the *Portrait of a Young Man* (possibly a self-portrait) already mentioned (at Hampton Court) with Roman buildings in the background also; the large *Cowper Madonna* in the National Gallery in Washington which is dated 1508. Also there is the upper part of the fresco in S. Severo in Perugia of the *Trinity and Saints*. Although a later manuscript dates it 1505, it is held to have been painted in 1507 or 1508, at the end of the Florentine period. The lower half was finished by Perugino.

Clearly then Raphael's work in these Florentine years was mainly the painting of pictures for private purchasers, Madonnas, Holy Families and portraits. The little known and foreign artist would have found it difficult to get commissions for large public works, or

◄ PLATE 16 - DISPUTE OVER THE HOLY SACRAMENT (C. 1509). DETAIL - VATICAN, STANZA OF THE SEGNATURA

orders from religious bodies, or works financed by private persons but destined for churches. Those he could get in Perugia where he was already known. In any case, it was better so, for Raphael was not compelled to scatter his talents in research for great monumental compositions, for which he was not yet ready. Indeed such works as the *Colonna Altar-piece* in New York and the *Ansidei Madonna* in London are not very felicitous, although the predella of the former has very delicate little scenes in it; nor is his Perugia work his best, where we feel the influence of Signorelli as well as that of Perugino. There was of course a splendid altar-piece of Signorelli's which Raphael could see in the cathedral at Perugia, which may have inspired him for the *Ansidei* altar-piece, especially for the Madonna on the throne intent on reading a book, since the figure on the right of the Signorelli altar-piece is a Saint Nicholas also reading. And the *Madonna del Baldacchino* may owe something to Fra Bartolomeo (as Gamba has pointed out) in the arrangement of a light-filled architectural scene, such as the friar had found and admired in the Giovanni Bellinis in Venice, and in a certain emphasis in various figures — which is not very admirable.

On the other hand superb achievements were to be obtained by Raphael in subsequent versions of the theme of the Madonna and Child, and of the Holy Family.

The *Madonna del Granduca* (PL. 8), dated by most to 1504-05, one of the earliest to be painted in Florence, was made on the orders of an unknown client. In the seventeenth century it belonged to the painter Carlo Dolci and in 1799 it was purchased by the Grand Duke Frederick III of Lorraine who was so enamoured of it that he used to take it with him even when travelling; hence its name.

An Uffizi drawing shows that this Madonna was first conceived in a tondo, probably with a landscape in the background, rather like the *Connestabile Madonna* (PL. 7) already mentioned. But thereafter, perhaps under the influence of Fra Bartolomeo Raphael did without background detail reducing it to pure shadow, and amplified the figures but with extreme sobriety (observe the garments with very few folds and devoid of embroidery). From

Leonardo he took his low tones, immersing the figures in a sort of luminous fluid, passing from full daylight to darkness, without violence. Hence his forms are at the same time large, solid and soft; all the hardness of plasticity and of linear outline of the Quattrocento has been abolished. At the same time there is a delicate modulation by imperceptible stages, both in the planes, in the faces, the bodies and the robes. The calm and sweet tone is further enhanced by the curvilinear rhythm in the heads, the limbs and especially the movement of the arms.

The Madonna and her Son are drawn with the simplicity of a modest young Florentine woman of the day, who comes out of the shadow with her own child. Raphael's marvellous simplification, amplification and sweetness also produce a classic effect by the idealisation of the natural. Thus in the *Madonna del Granduca* Christian divinity, tender and benevolent, is fully expressed in the Mother and in the Child.

And, moreover, the shape of the Virgin's figure, upright and enclosed from the knees upward, is fairly original. Figures like this are to be found in Perugino, but usually seated or kneeling. In the foreground, in front of the Virgin, there is nothing, not even the balustrades common to Giovanni Bellini's Madonnas. So Raphael's Madonna is seen with the majesty of the erect statue without the receding planes involved in seated or kneeling figures. Also the lower part of the body presents no problems since it does not have to rest on a defined base with the requisite perspectives that implies, as in the above-mentioned balustrades. Instead, the figure appears completely alone and with immediate effect in an effective but abstract space. This too is part of the idealisation, of the classicism, which Raphael, quietly and without showiness, worked out into really great forms.

In the *Madonna del Cardellino* in the Pitti (PL. 9) of about 1506, the Virgin and the two children are portrayed in front of a wide landscape and form a pyramidal mass. That doubtless happened under the influence of Leonardo's *Madonna and St Anne*. Instead of Leonardo's background of gigantic rocky mountains, Raphael has soft central-Italian hillsides, dotted with foreground slender trees, with a meadow on the left and a village in the distance. Above is a watery spring sky. The Virgin has stopped reading to listen, in a meditative and rather absent-minded way, to the two children, while they are playing with a small bird and exchanging glances which are rendered with much true observation of childish ways.

A gentle curved rhythm pervades the human group from the halo of the Virgin, her ovoid head and her bosom out to the ring formed by her arms, whose circle is completed by the two children. The forms seemingly posed with a natural placidity, really conform to a lucid geometric ideal, and much more so and more completely articulated than in the corresponding group by Leonardo; nor have the figures in the *Doni tondo* the twisted and emphasized plasticity of Michelangelo's *Holy Family*. In a word, Raphael is less romantic and sensitive than Leonardo; more sweet and serene than Michelangelo.

In the *Madonna im Gruenen* in Vienna, painted in 1506 possibly for Taddeo Taddei, who was an especially favoured client of Raphael's, the arrangement of the group is different, tending to be triangular in outline. But in the *Belle Jardinière* at the Louvre painted in 1507 the key point of the composition, being high up the sky's dome, is severed, and the group becomes more concentrated, with the kneeling John the Baptist looking up at the infant Jesus, who in turn looks up at his Mother. Hence the scale rises both formally and psychologically from the triangle to the spiral. Finally the *Canigiani Holy Family* has really too much virtuosity with the pyramid terminating in St Joseph, above a cross-play of diagonal glances.

Raphael's evolution as a portraitist is not less astonishing. Here Leonardo's formidable *Gioconda* must have entranced him, to judge by the already mentioned Louvre drawing (p. 36) from which the *Portrait of a Young Woman* in the Borghese Gallery in Rome (PL. 11) seems to derive.

This last was subsequently modified and transformed into a St Catherine, but in 1935 on Longhi's advice the original work was

DISPUTE OVER THE HOLY SACRAMENT (C. 1509) - VATICAN, STANZA OF THE SEGNATURA

restored, revealing a young woman with a unicorn, the symbol of chastity. Ortolani believes that this young lady is the real Maddalena Doni (who, according to Vasari was portrayed by Raphael, as was her husband). Ortolani held this view on the grounds that the Pitti portrait (PL. 13) of the Doni lady does not really portray Maddalena Strozzi in Doni at the tender age of sixteen or eighteen which she was at the time of Raphael's sojourn in Florence. He thought that the Pitti lady was her mother-in-law. But clearly the two Pitti portraits (PLS. 12 and 13) belong together, both in the pose of the subjects, the size and the similar landscape background.

53

Also they come from the Doni family who sold them to the Grand Duke of Tuscany in 1826. Would Raphael have painted mother and son and not not husband and wife as a pair?

The Borghese portrait is a doubtful attribution. It used to be ascribed to Perugino, then to Ridolfo Ghirlandaio or to Granacci. Certainly it is very clean, jewel-like, still, limpid and without that ample fluidity and that air of veiledness which the two Doni portraits at the Pitti have. Could it not be a work belonging to Raphael's earliest days in Rome?

As to the two Doni, Alazard once compared the *Gioconda* with the lady portrayed by Raphael (PL. 13). She has no visual fascination, possessing rather a hard expression in the lines of her mouth, and she displays the wealth of her dress and jewels (her medallion, the rings on her fat short fingers) in an ostentatious middle-class way. She is in fact faithfully rendered in her exterior, physical and social aspect, without any transfiguring sensitiveness. But, from a formal point of view the portrait is a splendid one; the human figure presides in an eloquent and ample setting; the rhythm of the volumes is broad and curved; the design is incisive and precise.

The male Doni portrait (PL. 12) when compared with Perugino's portraits, notably the *Francesco delle Opere* in the Uffizi, has an entirely new breadth. To attain this, Raphael used perspective (elsewhere rejected) by arranging the figure on several planes. Thus the red sleeves of the robe can be spread out, especially the left-hand one, which is nearer the viewer and becomes truly enormous, while the body between the two arms becomes a kind of small spatial shell, and as the eye travels round it up to the powerful head, it reaches the distances of the background, only to travel back along one of the arms to the projecting plane. Man dominates nature even though immersed in it.

According to Vasari, Angelo Doni gladly spent money on painting and sculpture ' especially when he was busily engaged in other things, for he took great delight in them, but was not extravagant about them '. He had been fortunate in getting Michelangelo to paint the *tondo* of the *Holy Family* (in the Uffizi) for his wedding to the

Countess Strozzi. But in Raphael's portrait he could not have found a better — even had he commissioned a Dürer or a Giorgione, at any price — to fix his and his wife's bourgeois features for posterity with greater dignity and indeed so economically.

Two other Raphael portraits must be mentioned. The *Gravida* at the Pitti, which gives a real impression of a woman awaiting with serenity the birth of her child, is held to be a little earlier than the two Doni portraits. The masterly expressiveness of the hands (which are not beholden to the *Gioconda* for their inspiration), the plain sombre background devoid of the landscape of those days, the absence of a certain Peruginesque oiliness and grimacery which is present in the Doni lady, could, on the other hand, indicate the contrary.

The *Muta* with similar features, in which Raphael again takes up the late fifteenth-century Florentine linear traditions of Botticelli and Ghirlandaio, is dated by Volpi 1507, rather than 1505. Certainly the *Muta's* rhythmical structure differs from the *Doni* portraits and is closer, if anything, to the Borghese portrait, but more sensitive. It is anterior, one would surmise, to the awful psychological twists on the faces in the early Pontormo portraits.

To quote Ortolani, it is not only in the *Muta* 'that the rhythmic function of the transverse line across space is obvious, as it gathers space into its invisible net and includes the ellipse which ideally contains the bust and the face, by following the curve of the two white puffs of linen revealed in the slits of the sleeves. If the index finger is pointing, it is doing so to indicate the whole outline which runs parallel from the line which falls off the right shoulder, and goes from the base of the other shoulder to the left-hand corner of the picture; while the two opposite diagonals correspond with this. These are rhymes and half rhymes of form answering each other, and peculiar to Raphael who knew how to make them into a continuous song'. Moreover the picture has solidly coordinated basic lines, marked almost invisibly by a series of accents: the vertical line made by the hair-parting, the profile of the nose, the slight extension of the chin down to the fall of the cross on the necklace on the breast; the horizontal and slightly oblique line in the small curvilinear flight of the eyebrows, the gloomy line of the lips, the fall of the shoulders and the path of the embroidered *décolleté*. There is therefore a nerve structure of architectural stability. But when the hands meet in the lower part of the picture, gone is the calm encounter of the *Doni* lady's portrait. Rather is the accent on opposing ramifications — almost a physical expression of mysterious spiritual lines which make a complicated knot in the still and secret melancholy of the face.

Raphael's *Deposition* (PL. 14) in the Borghese Gallery in Rome, formerly in Perugia, and dated 1507, belongs in its own special way to the Florentine period.

Violent local historical events are connected with the origins of this painting. On a July night in 1500, during a wedding feast, the young Grifonetto Baglioni together with some of his partisans had murdered four of his relations who had contested his right to rule the city. His cousin Giampaolo Baglioni, who had escaped the massacre, returned to the city two days later and in turn murdered Grifonetto. The latter's mother, Atalanta, had fled the day before with her daughter-in-law, condeming Grifonetto as a murderer and disowning him as a son. But when she heard of the new tragedy she rushed back with Grifonetto's wife and bad the dying man forgive his murderers. He did so, whereupon she gave him her blessing. When he was dead, the two women, bloodstained, passed through the crowd who made way for them respectfully. It was a pious wish of Atalanta to commemorate these events with a Deposition for the family chapel in San Francesco a Prato in Perugia. Grifonetto was no Christ, but the grief of Mary might portray her own grief as a just and Christian mother.

But it would be misleading to take Vasari's word that the Borghese *Deposition* ' represents the grief of the nearest and dearest relations who compose the body of a loved relative, in which act lies the wellbeing, the honour and the interest of a whole family '. The work is not full of sincerity and family mourning, but rather a very formal elaboration, eloquent and monumental, and in part clearly forced.

56

PLATE 17 - DISPUTE OVER THE HOLY SACRAMENT (C. 1509). DETAIL - VATICAN, STANZA OF THE SEGNATURA

PLATE 19 - DISPUTE OVER THE HOLY SACRAMENT (C. 1509). DETAIL - VATICAN, STANZA OF THE SEGNATURA

◀ PLATE 18 - DISPUTE OVER THE HOLY SACRAMENT (C. 1509). DETAIL - VATICAN, STANZA OF THE SEGNATURA

SCHOOL OF ATHENS (C. 1509-1510) - VATICAN, STANZA OF THE SEGNATURA

Long preparatory study for the work can be seen in at least sixteen drawings at Oxford, London (p. 65), Paris and Florence. One drawing at Oxford reveals how the *Deposition* was first conceived as ' grieving for the dead Christ ', in the manner of Perugino, and like his panel of 1495 in the Pitti (formerly in Santa Chiara) although Raphael had a different relationship between the figures, more flowing and less angular, with ample space above and open glimpses of the countryside round the human figures. All this is painted in a basic rhythm as of a drooping garland, apparent even in the final

◀ PLATE 20 - SCHOOL OF ATHENS (C. 1509-1510). DETAIL OF A SCRIBE - VATICAN, STANZA OF THE SEGNATURA

work. But that final work was to become a ' transfer to the sepulchre' (A. Venturi).

Here, in the final work, as Müntz noted, ' the scene is more
lively and complicated. Some are giving vent to their feelings while
others are carrying the body to the sepulchre which has been pre-
pared to receive it. The physical labour does in part replace the moral
suffering, and we must add, eventually relegates it to second place '.
Another drawing in the British Museum (p. 65) illustrates the second
conception and depicts the two Marys joining in the procession to
the sepulchre and not, as in final version, a procession halted, because
the Madonna has fainted.

The *Deposition*, as Adolfo Venturi writes, ' by arranging the
head and body of Christ and the head and body of Nicodemus down
a single inclined plane compels the eye to that dark cave which is
about to envelop the corpse, almost with the force of a creaking cable
drawing the body slowly up to the height of the sepulchre. Here
Raphael expresses the maximum energy expressed during his Florentine period, nor was it achieved without much labour on the part
of the gentle painter. As a counterbalance, the young man who holds
up the far piece of the shroud steps backwards, and in so doing reveals
his archangelic beauty... and it is this opposition of forces, and in
this image of Mary kneeling near the Virgin and turning on her knees
like that Micheangelesque virago in the *tondo* of the *Holy Family*,
that we realize how the champion sculptor of Florence has fascinated
Raphael into his own orbit. But the revolving movement of the woman
in the *Deposition* happens suavely... Upon the shroud... Christ lies
as in a hammock: and the arc of the figures which dips towards
the bending figure of Mary Magdalen in its centre, brings to mind
again a shell; the white clouds in the sky, the hills and the decliv-
ities on the earth repeat the rhythms of the group...'

The Christ of the *Pietà* in St Peter's by Michelangelo seems to
have been the model for the Christ in the *Deposition*, though how
Raphael could have seen it I do not know: and something of Michelangelo's head of David seems to have passed to the head of the
bearer on the right of the *Deposition*, yet these references to Michel-

angelo of themselves cannot explain the *Deposition*. That painting is different from and something more than the Michelangelo manner. Raphael's classicism has another spirit and another harmony — also heroic but more moderate and more human, monumental and eloquent, but with a softer, ampler and more relaxed rhythm. The *Deposition* presages not only Raphael's work in Rome but a great deal of subsequent interpretation of Classicism which the Caracci, Poussin and David will adopt, under the influence of its deep, ample spaciousness.

The originality and grandeur of the *Deposition* is not derived from Michelangelo. The originality of the composition is based on the balance of two different masses of figures, the first obliquely mounting in a play of contrasts and concordances from the left side, and the second arranged vertically in the second plane on the right. And as we said, the eye travels along down and up this chain of figures from the two bearers, and into the depths of the painting and out again to the surface. From the distant hill with the three crosses down to the sepulchre on the left, the whole path of the *Deposition*, the landscape and the human figures of the drama are worked into the rhythm of the composition.

Raphael interpreted the Michelangelo manner in his original way (possibly inspired by the *St Matthew* of Buonarroti) in his *St Catherine* in London; a calm and sweet figure despite the twists and turns of her body. She has a preparatory drawing at the Louvre. It has more pathos than the painting, by virtue of the deep shadows.

But to go back to the *Deposition* — in it, only three years after the *Sposalizio* at the Brera, Raphael could date and sign in Perugia this capital work, so fundamental for the history of painting in Italy and in the world. Bembo was not exaggerating when he called Raphael ' the great master of painting ' in a letter of 1507. Nevertheless Raphael the man remained a simple and practical person. So we found him in a letter he wrote to his uncle in 1508, and now, in a signed letter attached to a drawing in Lille, we find him asking his colleague Domenico Alfani, ' do ask the lady Atalanta Baglioni to send me the money, and really tell the watchmaker Cesarino in Perugia that he could remind her and ask for it...'

It seems that sometime in 1508 Raphael suddenly left Florence and was called to Rome by Pope Julius II. Bramante appears to have advised the Pope to summon him, and Bramante may have been distantly related to Raphael. Another recommendation may have come from the young Francesco Maria della Rovere, a nephew both of Julius II and of Guidobaldo, whom he had just succeeded in the Dukedom of Urbino.

There is a letter dated September 5, 1508 written from Rome to France by Raphael and published by Malvasia in the seventeenth century, but now believed to be false. But on October 4, 1509 Julius II confirmed Raphael as 'painter of the palace'. By then the Urbino painter was probably already engaged on the frescoes of the Vatican Halls, whereas his name does not appear with those of Sodoma, Bramante and Lotto until March of the preceeding year. But their work in those Stanze, like that of Perugino, Peruzzi and earlier Masters like Piero della Francesca, Signorelli and Bartolomeo della Gatta had disappeared, except for some ceiling decoration, to give place to the work of the new Master: and Sodoma and Lotto, as we shall see, may simply have had to rest content with assisting him in some details.

Raphael was to spend the next twelve years of his life in Rome, until his death in 1520. They were to be twelve years filled with glory and used in a vast series of labours. Let us briefly recall the scene, the atmosphere and the men among whom the Master's last and greatest period was spent.

Rome then — the city — was the living symbol of Antiquity, presently in the process of being mythicized by the Renaissance into its highest ideal. And, with the revival in the fortunes of the Papacy and the flowering of Italian civilization, Rome boasted alongside the great vestiges of its past history, the signs of a contemporary activity which truly seemed to vie with its past political and artistic greatness. The foundations of the new St Peter's must have looked something like the huge ancient ruins. The adventurous and warlike policy of Julius II was shaking all Italy, threatening to involve her in a perilous international game, which would shortly spell ruin.

STUDY FOR THE DISPUTE OVER THE HOLY SACRAMENT (C. 1509) - FRANKFURT-ON-MAIN
STADEL INSTITUTE

ADAM - FLORENCE, UFFIZI DRAWINGS CABINET ▶

STUDY FOR THE MASSACRE OF THE INNOCENTS (C. 1509) - WINDSOR CASTLE

PLATE 2I - SCHOOL OF ATHENS (C. 1509-1510). DETAIL OF EPICURUS - VATICAN ▶
STANZA OF THE SEGNATURA

PLATE 23 - SCHOOL OF ATHENS. DETAIL OF ARISTOTLE

◀ PLATE 22 - SCHOOL OF ATHENS. DETAIL OF DELLA ROVERE

But the slogan 'Out with the Barbarians!' directed against the French, whose entry into Italy under Charles VIII was largely due to Julius II when he was still a Cardinal, was of clearly Roman inspiration, like a spark of the old Italian fire.

So, after the small and choice Urbino, came the great centre and cradle of the Renaissance that was Florence, and now Rome offered Raphael a much larger spiritual horizon, a vision as vast and as high as could be imagined: from the wide outlines and the solemn air of Rome's solitary landscape to the dreams conjured up by the great Roman remains; from the uninterrupted documentation of all Italian Christian art offered by the monuments of centuries, down to the newest undertakings which the genius of Julius II rendered viable.

About 1519 Raphael had been engaged on a great plan of ancient Rome for the reigning Pope Leo X. He accompanied it with a letter, which is in itself a preface, saying: 'Many people, Holy Father, when observing the great relics of the Romans, their armaments, their city of Rome, its marvellous artifice, riches, ornaments and great buildings, lamely judge them fabulous rather than real. But with me the experience is different, for as I consider the many remains which one still sees in the ruins of Rome, and the inspiration of those ancient souls, I think it not unreasonable that many things which appear impossible to us, seemed very easy to them'. Thus he wrote in a letter to Leo X about 1519 even if we have to read it in the elegant language of Castiglione.

There are two other sentiments in this letter; on the one hand 'seeing what is almost the corpse of this noble soul of a city, once queen of the world, now so sorely reduced' by the hand of Christian and barbarian who had helped themselves to the antiquities whenever they needed material for new constructions; and on the other hand the request to the Pontiff to preserve what was left: 'let Your Holiness preserve the paragon of the monuments of the ancients, even while you equal and excel them as you do with magnificent buildings, favouring and nourishing their virtues and reawakening inventive genius by rewarding good labour and spreading the sacred spirit of peace among Christian princes...'

◀ PLATE 24 - SCHOOL OF ATHENS (C. 1509-1510). DETAIL OF HERACLITUS - VATICAN, STANZA OF THE SEGNATURA

And besides the City and the two Pontiffs — the giant Julius II and the intensely refined Leo X — so different and both strikingly magnanimous, what other circles were there at that time in Rome which might encourage the genius and arouse the energies of Raphael?

Cardinal Pietro Bembo, the famous humanist, would be his friend. One day together they made an excursion to Tivoli with two Venetian writers, Navagero and Beazzano, later to be jointly portrayed by Raphael (the picture is in the Doria Gallery in Rome today). Bembo mentioned the painter several times in letters to his colleague Bibbiena, and it was Bembo who composed Raphael's epitaph in the Pantheon.

It is possible that the well-known, worldly and witty Cardinal Bibbiena had got to know Raphael at Urbino and he may have played a part in getting Julius II to invite Raphael to come to Rome. A close friendship was to grow up between the Cardinal and the painter, as shown in Raphael's work for him: the Cardinal's portrait in the Pitti, the decoration of the Bibbiena chimney-piece in the Vatican, the *Giovanna d'Aragona* in the Louvre. There is too a letter of 1515 from Cardinal Bembo to Bibbiena asking for a statue, and Raphael supports the request: 'If by any chance you think my request too bold, Raphael whom you love says he will make my excuses to you'. Bibbiena actually wanted to have Raphael in his family, and gave him his niece Maria in marriage, but the artist being otherwise engaged let the matter drag on, and nothing came of it. The plan ended with the early death of the young woman.

In the Curia was a literary bishop *Fedra* (?) *Inghirami* whom Raphael painted about 1513-16. The original is in the Isabella Gardner Museum in Boston, and a replica possibly by Raphael in the Pitti (PL. 36); there was also Bishop Luigi di Canossa for whom Raphael designed the *Madonna della Perla*, formerly in the Canossa Palace in Verona, now in Madrid.

The private secretary of Julius II, Sigismondo Conti of Foligno was painted by Raphael in his *Madonna di Foligno* (PL. 30), kneeling in gratitude at having been spared when a piece of a meteor fell on his house in that city. The episode is depicted in the background of the painting. The president of the Chancellery, Baldassare Turini of Pescia was one of Raphael's Executors and purchased the unfinished *Madonna del Baldacchino* for a church in his native city. The suppliants' clerk at the Vatican, Jean Goritz of Luxemburg, commissioned Raphael to do the fresco of *Isaiah* in S Agostino in Rome. Cardinal Colonna commissioned the *S Giovannino* which is in the Gallery of the Florence Academy today, and was painted by Raphael's assistants. Cardinal Lorenzo Pucci commissioned the *St Cecily and other Saints* in Bologna today. Bishop Gianozzo Pandolfini ordered Raphael to design his palace in the Via San Gallo in Florence. Then there was Giovan Battista Branconio dell'Aquila for whom Raphael designed a fine palace in the Borgo and also painted the *Visitation*, now in the Prado.

Among Raphael's lay friends was Baldassar Castiglione, that learned and gentlemanly figure who gave the painter much cultural information and collaborated with him, as we have seen, in the preface to the Map of ancient Rome. In about 1515 Raphael painted his noble features for eternity in his portrait *Baldassar Castiglione* (PL. 39), now in the Louvre — which struck Rembrandt because of its admirable colours and the expressive concentration of its form.

The infamous Pietro Aretino would boast that he counselled Chigi to assign the decoration of his villa to Raphael. That rich and powerful banker Agostino Chigi commissioned Raphael to paint not only the *Galatea* (PL. 31) and the frescoes of *Cupid and Psyche* in the Farnesina, but also the *Sybils and the Angels* in the Chapel of Santa Maria della Pace in Rome. In his will dated 1519, Agostino Chigi asked that Raphael should finish the decoration of his chapel in S Maria del Popolo, which had been architecturally designed by Raphael, who also made the model for the *Jonah* which Lorenzetto subsequently carved in marble, as well as the design for the mosaics in the ceiling in Santa Maria.

Raphael also painted another young, proud banker-patron, *Bindo Altoviti* (PL. 38) formerly in Munich, now in Washington, which Venturi describes as ' an elegant figure with glassy eyes and

PARNASSUS (1511) - VATICAN, STANZA OF THE SEGNATURA

hair like handfuls of spun silk, fair and soft'. It is a bust seen from an unusual angle, from the side and over the shoulder, while the head is three-quarters facing the viewer. For Altoviti Raphael also painted the *Madonna dell'Impannata* in the Pitti.

Princes like the young Della Rovere, his mother the Prefect's wife whom we have already met, the reigning Isabella d'Este from Mantua, a great patron of the arts, and Duke Alfonso of Ferrara all came to Rome from time to time and all were in touch with Raphael.

Other famous artists were working in Rome at the same time: we have named several beginning with Bramante, the introducer and protector of Raphael, who nominated him as his successor in the

PLATE 26 - PARNASSUS (1511). DETAIL - VATICAN, STANZA OF THE SEGNATURA

PLATE 27 - PARNASSUS (1511). DETAIL - VATICAN, STANZA OF THE SEGNATURA ▶

PLATE 28 - PORTRAIT OF A CARDINAL (C. 1510-1511) - MADRID, PRADO

post of architect of St Peter's and we shall name others also. But we must here make some reference to the fierce competition between Raphael and Michelangelo.

The latter, as Leo X remarked, had a difficult temperament. He complained that Bramante's protege and fellow-citizen was proud, resentful and full of persecution mania. Michelangelo had said the same of Bramante, earlier. And what a day it must have been when Bramante suggested to Julius II that the second half of the Sistine ceiling should be painted by Raphael! The two were of opposite character: Michelangelo solitary, difficult, cursory, extremely proud; Raphael cheerful, accommodating, very benevolent towards his pupils. Lomazzo tells the anecdote that Raphael was one day walking with his pupils, 'when he met Michelangelo who asked him', "Where are you going surrounded like a general?", to which Raphael replied "And you, alone, like an executioner?"

Two schools began to grow up in Rome, the gay and flourishing school of Raphael who was fast becoming the leader of the city, the other of his adversaries led by the bitter Sebastiano del Piombo, who quoted Michelangelo's work as the basis of their criticism. They accused Raphael of being no more than an imitator of Michelangelo's art: Raphael's admirers replied that Raphael's colours, his invention and grace were superior, and that only in draftsmanship could Michelangelo compete.

On January I, 1518, a certain Leonardo Sellaio wrote to Michelangelo about the *Story of Cupid and Psyche* in the Farnesina: 'The ceiling of Agostino Chigi has been unveiled; it is an insult by a great artist, worse than the last room of the palace, by far, so that Bastian [Sebastiano del Piombo] fears nothing. You should know about this'. On July 2 of the same year Sebastiano himself wrote to his protector Michelangelo: 'I think Leonardo has told you all about my affairs and how slow my work is and unfinished [the reference is to the *Resurrection of Lazarus* in London which Sebastiano was painting, seeking to rival Raphael's *Transfiguration*]; I have been so slow that I don't want Raphael to see my picture, while he has not finished his, and for this I have the promise of the most reverend Cardinal [Giuliano dei Medici, later Pope Clement VII], who has often been to my house... I am truly sorry you haven't been to Rome to see the two pictures by the prince of the synagogue [Raphael] which have gone to France, for you could not imagine works more contrary to your view, than these. I can only say they seem humbug to me, or like wrought iron figures, drawn in a way Leonardo will describe to you... Please get Domenico to agree to gild the panel in Rome, and to let me do the gilding for I want to prove to the Cardinal that Raphael steals at least three ducats a day from the pope on the days he gilds...'

Alongside this slander, it is as well to remember the story of how Michelangelo, when asked one day to estimate a price for the *Sybils* painted by Raphael for Agostino Chigi, named a price double of that proposed by Chigi's accountant, and Raphael himself, we shall see, declared his admiration for the great Florentine, even publicly.

Here we must pass to other matters and especially to the women in Raphael's life, for a temperament like Raphael's, which to us appears psychologically happy, could not but provide him with a warm, indeed a too warm, admiration for women. In a sonnet sequence (at which he now tries his hand, making up for a scanty literary activity in the past) scribbled out on some drawings for the *Dispute over the Holy Sacrament* and therefore written about 1509 at the beginning of his Rome period, Raphael voices an amorous passion: later he was to become involved in many adventures, among which the famous love affair with the Fornarina, who has been identified as Margherita, daughter of Francesco Luti, a baker in the Roman district of Santa Dorotea. The lady appears, half nude, in a portrait in the Borghese Gallery, a studio painting however. She appears again, richly dressed, in the portrait *La Velata* (PL. 41) in the Pitti, in which the sleeve in the foreground is painted with a sumptuous richness, like a hymn of praise to the beauty of the material.

Lastly, we must remember the palace built by Bramante which Raphael purchased in 1517. He was to buy other properties later. This one was a gigantic studio full of old curiosities. One recalls a passage in Vasari: 'So considerable was the greatness of this man, that his draftsmen were scattered all over Italy, down to Pozzuolo and even to Greece; and at home he kept everything necessary to his art'. All his drawings and those of his very numerous pupils filled the studio. We know enough now to understand his proud but affectionate and human letter of 1514 to his uncle, Simone Ciarla: ' Up to the present time I find I have things worth three thousand ducats in gold in Rome, and an income of fifty thousand crowns... and then I am paid for work I like to do, and I have begun painting another hall for His Holiness, which will bring me twelve hundred gold ducats: so that, dear uncle, I do honour to you and to all our relations and to the homeland, but I always carry you in my heart, and when I hear you mentioned, it is as though they were talking of my father'.

Raphael's work in the Vatican began with the fresco-ing of one of the rooms in the apartments of Julius II who would not live in the rooms previously occupied by his ill-famed predecessor and enemy, Alexander VI. Julius chose to live in the older part of the palace built by Pope Nicholas III and later altered by Pope Nicholas V. It was thought that Julius wanted the room as a library, but its smallness and the fact that all the walls were to be frescoed by Raphael makes this unlikely. The room received the name of Stanza della Segnatura, and the Ecclesiastical Tribunal indeed held its sittings there. This first cycle of paintings belongs to the period 1508 to the end of 1511.

The cycle is inspired by a complicated intellectual plan emanating from the literary people in the Papal Court or from the Pope himself. It celebrates three neoplatonist ' categories ' which were fashionable then: the True, the Good and the Beautiful. The True is treated in its supernatural form in a medallion on the ceiling of *Theology*, and in its natural form in the rectangular representation of *Adam and Eve*, originators of the *felix culpa*, followed by the coming of Christ, which reveals the whole of supernatural truth. This is in the large lunette below the so-called *Dispute over the Holy Sacrament* or the *Triumph of the Christian Religion*. To illustrate the Good are *Philosophy* on the ceiling, *Astronomy* in the rectangular

EXPULSION OF HELIODORUS (1511-1512) - VATICAN, STANZA OF HELIODORUS

lunette beneath, below *The School of Athens*. Then, to correspond with the category of the Good, there is the medallion of *Justice*, and again the rectangular fresco of the *Judgment of Solomon*, the lunette with the cardinal and theological virtues (the principles which suggest the Good); and below, on each side of a window in the wall, *Gregory IX approving the Decretals* and *Justinian publishing the Pandects* — to show that the Law is canonical as well as civil. On the last wall opposite this one, which also has a window, the Beautiful is represented by *Poetry, Apollo and Marsyas*, the *Parnassus*, and two chiaroscuros showing *Augustus preventing the burning of the Aeneid* and *Alexander the Great ordering the placing of the Homeric books on the tomb of Achilles*.

PLATE 29 - EXPULSION OF HELIODORUS (1511-1512). DETAIL - VATICAN, STANZA OF HELIODORUS

page 86: PLATE 30 - MADONNA DI FOLIGNO (1511-1512) - VATICAN, GALLERY

page 87: PLATE 31 - TRIUMPH OF GALATEA (1512) - ROME, FARNESINA

PLATE 32 - MIRACLE AT BOLSENA (1512-1513). DETAIL - VATICAN, STANZA OF HELIODORUS

MIRACLE AT BOLSENA (1512-1513) - VATICAN, STANZA OF HELIODORUS

But of course it is the formal language of these subjects in the Stanza of the Segnatura which is of the greatest interest. In the four ceiling medallions from the highest to the lowest in the usual order of a fresco painting, we probably see the first Vatican paintings of Raphael. Traits of Michelangelo are certainly present especially in *Justice*, more reminiscent than the others of the Madonna in the *Doni tondo* of Michelangelo, where the nude figures in the background remind one of the putti of the medallion, and especially the one on the left which holds the inscription ' Jus suum ', and the one on the right with its body seen in profile. The former is comparable with the S. Giovannino on the right of the *Doni tondo* in the middle background.

The anatomic vigour of the figures in the rectangular frescoes also recall Michelangelo. Yet one only has to compare Raphael's *Adam and Eve* with the Adam and Eve which Michelangelo was at that very time engaged upon painting, in secret, in the Sistine Chapel, to see how remote was the vision of a primogenital titanism at which Michelangelo had arrived, from Raphael's measured, human, classical, elegant, sensitive and carefully descriptive conception. Raphael's woodland scene in the earthly paradise compared with Michelangelo's violent and economic treatment of the same subject, is an example. Not on this account does Raphael fail to create effects of considerable suggestiveness, even if the form of communication is simplified, as in his *Astronomy* where the figure is bent in examination of the map of the heavens, with the left hand raised as though to signify the first creative act. Michelangelo would have been unable to achieve such a composition or to have designed the map so finely, but Raphael knew how to submit himself to a figurative language which corresponded perfectly with the concepts of his patrons and would be easily understood by the public. The early Renaissance tradition of elegant adaptability to given contents, as seen in the Vatican itself, in Pollaiolo's tombs of Sixtus IV and Innocent VIII with their allegorical figures, or in the detailed ornamentation of Pinturicchio's frescoes in the Borgia apartments, would have assisted Raphael in this.

Michelangelo's tendency to a grandiose synthesis came to him by way of his vision as a sculptor who would inevitably concentrate on the human figure, while Raphael in the Vatican halls was to exemplify the infinitely wide illustrative possibilities of painting, such as Leonardo had claimed for the art, and such as dominated the whole argument, very fashionable in the Cinquecento, about whether sculpture or painting was supreme. Leonardo had in fact written: ' the painter is master of all that can occur in the thought of a man... in fact the universe, its essence, its presence, its imagination is in the mind and then in the brush of painting, and is of such excellence that a harmonious proportion is made in a single creative perception...' In Rome Raphael's art was indeed intent on achieving 'the universe, its essence, its presence and its imagination' — in fact any human concept whatsoever, general or particular, was to be expressed 'with harmonious proportion' through 'the mind' and with 'the brush'.

This fundamental characteristic of Raphael's art was grasped by Vasari: he saw that Raphael had overcome Perugino's manner by his study of Michelangelo (passing in fact from a more detailed to a more grandiose measure, from an art already surpassed to one that was the most contemporary conceivable), but that he had also succeeded in leaving the dangerous orbit of Michelangelo, in which so many Mannerists became transfixed. In his own sphere Michelangelo was insuperable, but (as Vasari put it) 'painting does not consist merely in making nudes. It has a wider field and among perfect painters are those who can express, well and easily, all the inventions in a story and its many deviations with a fine judgment... Raphael resolved these problems, for Michelangelo could add nothing where Raphael had painted even if in other spheres Raphael would have liked to vie with him or excel him. So Raphael devoted himself not to imitating his manner, thereby losing time in vain, but in making himself a universal master of these other parts (stories, landscapes etc) which are there told'.

Raphael fashioned this 'universal' art of his according to an exceedingly noble formalism which could make a synthesis of his greatest contemporary figurative artists, of Perugino, the Florentines, Leonardo, Michelangelo and even the Venetians. He could achieve the synthesis with a harmonious moderation peculiar to himself. This is the real key for appreciating all his work in the Vatican Stanze, some of it sublime indeed.

These frescoes are so famous and have been so often reproduced and exalted by critics that, after examining one of them as one might a book, we can proceed more briefly and refer back. In any case great masterpieces possess a convincing power and an ever-present validity in their values, such as to render superfluous, and even annoying and vacuous and vulgar, much further elucidation.

The *Dispute over the Holy Sacrament* (page 53 and PL. 15-19) portrays the Trinity in the sky surrounded by angelic throngs, Mary and the Baptist by the side of Christ and a semicircle of patriarchs and prophets of the Old Testament and apostles and martyrs of the New; St Peter and Adam, St John the Evangelist and David etc. This is the Church triumphant. Beneath and around the altar (adorned with Leonardesque patterns) with its consecrated Host as the link between earth and heaven, stands the Church militant, the Fathers and Doctors of the Church, some of whom bear the features of well-known contemporaries of Raphael. A lean Dominican on the left is Fra Angelico; the man leaning on the balustrade and pointing to a book is Bramante; the blond young man (PL. 16) in yellow and blue robes pointing at the altar is Julius II's nephew, Francesco Maria della Rovere; then, towards the centre, the Pope on the throne with the 'Liber Moralium'; at his feet is St Gregory the Great, but with the face of Julius II; and in the right-hand group the hawk-like face of Dante is unmistakable, standing behind the erect figure of Pope Sixtus IV; alongside stands a figure that looks like an ancient Zeus, and then, shrouded in his hood, Savonarola the victim of Alexander VI, but held in great esteem by Julius II. In the same area there seems to be an allusion to the foundations of the throne of St Peter, and the huge block on the right appears to resemble a part of it, such as Bramante designed — like a gigantic ancient ruin.

Here is past and present, theology, history and contemporary chronicle. Heaven and Earth co-exist in the fresco, in accordance with typical Italian fourteenth and especially fifteenth-century taste. Tradition and culture cohabit, even in the very composition which was such an extraordinary innovation. It is usual to compare the upper part of the Church triumphant with Fra Bartolomeo's *Last Judgment*, now in the San Marco Museum, and with Fra Angelico's *Judgment*, also there, but celestial Glorias arranged in a semicircle can be traced back to mediaeval mosaics in the apse or even to palaeo-

PLATE 34 - MIRACLE AT BOLSENA (1512-1513). DETAIL - VATICAN, STANZA OF HELIODORUS

PLATE 35 - MIRACLE AT BOLSENA (1512-1513). DETAIL - VATICAN, STANZA OF HELIODORUS

PLATE 36 - PORTRAIT OF TOMASO INGHIRAMI, CALLED FEDRA (C. 1513-1514)
FLORENCE, PITTI GALLERY

christian apses in which the semicircle was a kind of natural and perspective adjustment. From Fra Bartolomeo Raphael had already borrowed when he painted his fresco in S. Severo in Perugia, by arranging his saints in two short wings on either side of Christ. A more direct and convincing precedent for the semicircular arrangement in the *Dispute* as in the *School of Athens* could be found in Bramante. Has not the semicircular niche of the Belvedere a similar spatial breadth, equally inspired by ancient Roman architecture?

This upper part of the *Dispute* stands by itself, enclosed at the summit as it were by the golden veil of the aureole of angels. The Trinity stands in a forward position and above the semicircle, and the severed figures are clearly passing behind it. Christ sits almost like a Roman emperor at the circus, separated even from the foremost row of the highest officials. Between the small clouds at the base of the aureole of angels and the cloudy base of the semicircle, a great sky opens behind the seated personages of the Church triumphant, and hangs wide over the earth on which the adoration of the Host takes place. Here is a gathering as in a Council, of theologians of every century, some adoring, some meditating, pointing, discussing, writing down (PLS. 15-19).

This bringing-to-life again of an old idealized Academy, even before the painting of the *School of Athens*, was surely a great innovation. Where before had such a sacred gathering been conceived, disposed in active and not merely ecstatic groups, with such vital autonomy in each single participant? Possibly a source can be found in Leonardo's circle of people, kneeling moved, stretched out around the Madonna and Child in his *Adoration of the Magi* in the Uffizi, or in the psychological animation of his *Last Supper* in Milan, which Raphael might have know about indirectly. Then there is a preparatory sketch in Frankfurt (p. 66) with nude figures, a study for the composition of the *Dispute* in anatomical form only, which shows another source besides Michelangelo, as indeed Venturi has pointed out, and that source may be Luca Signorelli. The latter's *Paradise* in Orvieto Cathedral certainly seems the direct source of the back view of the nude figure.

There are other aspects of the composition of the *Dispute*: the spreading out from the vertical central axis of a circle, from the Host to the halo of the Holy Spirit on to the great gold disc before which Christ sits; and again the way the lines whirl in semicircles first with the angels above, then in the Church triumphant, then again ideally along the two groups of the Church militant. One can see too how Raphael was possessed of a new vision in which ' the spatial arrangement is no longer based on the flat geometry of quattrocento perspective, but on what might be called a spherical geometry ' (Salvini).

Just this kind of perspective implies, on the one hand, setting the human figure within curvilinear schemes because they have a centralizing quality, and, on the other, an intensification of the surrounding spaciousness so that, as in the *Dispute*, it spreads out in circles towards infinity. In quattrocento perspective, man was basically the measure of the imagined reality of the picture regardless of the area of the painting, while the geometric centre of that reality was a perspective in depth. So in the end space came to be the chief internal subject, and man the external subject. But in Raphael's new vision the human figure occupies a preeminent position, geometrically central to the whole composition. All the surrounding reality converges upon it. The role of the outside observer loses its somewhat detached nature when faced with this new dignity of man, inherent in the composition. He is now drawn into the whole fiction of art and sustained by a familiar vision free of incident — ideal, universal and classical. Salvini says: ' As in Bramante's architecture, so here man has become the centre of the universe, the pivot round which the everlasting skies revolve. This space bears no relation to that real space occupied by the spectator, as it used to in quattrocento perspective. It now soars in a more detached and higher sphere... the volumes of the figures exist in this high and ample space with full plasticity, softened however by a subtle gradation of Leonardonesque quality, which easily avoids any defined limit and naturally merges into the space. There is between space and figures a relation of continuous and complex rhythms, governed by supreme harmony '.

In the second of these two sublime and enormous moon-shaped pendent frescoes, the *School of Athens* (page 61 and PLS. 20-24) a vision of a basilica is suggested, as in ancient Roman architecture, or indeed in Bramante who is said to have provided Raphael with the design for this superb perspective, much as Brunelleschi did in the case of St Maria Novella with Masaccio. Here the architecture encloses and exalts the human circle in a solemn spatial envelope, and the great rhythm seems to proceed in majestically full, calm, slow waves, from the architecture down the breakwater of the first groups of learned figures.

Among these Plato (in the guise of Leonardo?) pointing to the heavens and Aristotle to the earth, dominate the central axis, framed as they are in the last archway (of the succession of archways in depth which forms the geometrical motive of the *School of Athens*). Each figure in turn is wonderfully drawn: a dyonisiac and colourful Epicurus (PL. 21); the tender beauty of a figure representing the young Della Rovere (PL. 22); the sudden passionate turning upward of a head in the group (PL. 20) in which Euclid is bending over a slate, is a new homage to, and portrait of, Bramante.

In the only surviving drawing for the fresco, in the Ambrosiana Gallery in Milan, the portraits of Raphael and Sodoma which were inserted on the extreme right, are missing. Heraclitus (PL. 24), pensive and stylistically certainly a most formal tribute to Michelangelo, is also absent from the drawing. Half of Michelangelo's Sistine ceiling had been unveiled in August, 1511, to the wonder and admiration of everyone. Redig De Campos suggests that the head is a true portrait of Michelangelo. Rival as he was of Michelangelo, Raphael proved his chivalry by this tribute, and it was kind to introduce Sodoma alongside, for Sodoma had been decorating the same room before Raphael. Nor was it necessary, as some have maintained, to equalize the two groups by introducing the figure of Heraclitus — for they were already quite balanced in the drawing in spite of certain variations: two standing figures on the outside of the semicircle and two erect on the inside.

LIBERATION OF ST PETER (1514) - VATICAN, STANZA OF HELIODORUS

The *Parnassus* (page 76 and PLS. 25-27) clearly suffers from the presence of the window in the centre of the wall; but it certainly posesses an upward rhythm which is also circular, coming from each side of the apex. There is genius in this, and the apex itself has spiritual significance. There is a lyric atmosphere in the dreamy softness of the figures, and their postures, carefully arranged, seem almost to symbolize the formal and elegant exercise of the arts.

Another splendid creation of Raphael which belongs to 1511 is the *Galatea* (PL. 31) which he painted for Chigi in the Farne-

PLATE 37 - LIBERATION OF ST PETER (1514). DETAIL - VATICAN, STANZA OF HELIODORUS

PLATE 38 - PORTRAIT OF BINDO ALTOVITI - WASHINGTON, NATIONAL GALLERY

PLATE 39 - PORTRAIT OF BALDASSAR CASTIGLIONE (C. 1514-1515) - PARIS, LOUVRE

PLATE 40 - MADONNA DELLA SEGGIOLA (C. 1514-1516) - FLORENCE, PITTI GALLERY

sina. The inspiration is classical and the ancient myth comes warmly, fantastically and sensitively to life again in the interweaving and opposing movements, and in the twisting spiral of the forms. A few figures boldly occupy the seascape. The contemporary *Madonna di Foligno* (PL. 30) though it is impaired by traces of pietistic unction, marks the earliest contacts with the Venetian world, especially if, as is generally believed, the two Dossi brothers had a hand in it. They were Giorgionesque painters of Ferrara, and in Rome at that time.

But it was especially Raphael's contact with the hostile Sebastiano del Piombo, who had moved from Venice to Rome in 1511, and possibly with Lorenzo Lotto, already painting frescoes in the Vatican (now lost) in 1509, which enriched his art with a new great experience of Venetian colour tones. This is very noticeable in the Stanza of Heliodorus (1511-14). 'In the *Segnatura* the concept and theme are spiritual; here they are, in the highest sense, political, in that the scene presents us with God's protection of the faithful from the most ancient of times' (Camesasca). In fact the ceiling bears the legends *The Burning Bush, Jacob's Ladder, God appearing to Noah, The Sacrifice of Isaac,* while the titles in the large lunettes are *The Expulsion of Heliodorus, The Mass of Bolsena, The Arrest of Attila, The freeing of St Peter.* The figure of Pope Julius II is painted in the first two of these great scenes; in the third his successor Pope Leo X appears, since Julius II had died in 1513, and oddly enough he appears twice, as Raphael had already painted him in the guise of a cardinal in the same fresco.

The four ceiling scenes in their dramatic propulsion carry the mark of Michelangelo's influence. The *Expulsion of Heliodorus* (page 84 and PL. 29) into a void which cuts through two groups — the one on the left in which the Pope appears, with the women horrified at the three divine wreakers of vengeance on Heliodorus and his brigands over on the right — is dramatic too. By contrast with the solemn calm of the architecture and the serenity of the light in the *School of Athens*, here, (as Adolfo Venturi writes) ' complex groups of columns and half columns, flat and convex surfaces appear in the temple which rises like scenery; the light is now glowing, now spent; the architectural idea changes; the rhythm of light and shade, like that of the composition, grows faster; the ancient serenity of atmosphere and of form gives way to a romantic sense of struggle. From cupola to cupola reddish, tempestuous and ever more threatening strokes of lightning pursue each other as they approach the angels who are chasing those fleeing from them. The gold flashes light up the aisles like funeral lights in the shadows of a crypt '. Raphael may owe much to Venice in the Stanza of Heliodorus, but he quickly repaid the debt in the way he showered the light on the architecture and especially in the high inventiveness of the two figures perching on the column base, which anticipates Tintoretto, if one thinks of his famous *Finding of St Mark's Body*.

In the *Miracle at Bolsena* (page 89 and PLS. 32-35) the story of a miracle of 1263 is told, which was the origin of the institution of the Feast of Corpus Cristi, and of the foundation of the Cathedral of Orvieto. A priest from Bohemia on his way to Rome was suddenly seized with doubts about whether there was such a thing as transubstantiation, just as he was celebrating the mass on the tomb of St Christina in Bolsena. A few drops of blood then appeared on the Host. A Raphael School drawing at Oxford shows how Raphael had first conceived his fresco of the event with the Papal group on the left, instead of on the right, with a bigger crowd on the opposite side, while the priest was to be celebrating the mass against a semicircular background of architectural niches. But there was a door, and not even a central one, in the wall, so that Raphael already in the drawing used this impediment as a support for his high altar, to which side steps ascended.

The pediment thus gave an added importance to the scene and to the chief actors. In the fresco the Pope was directly in front of the priest, but not so in the drawing.

The romantic element is strong. Raphael's new chromatic and tonal richness contributes to it: the sky beyond the portico is streaked with silvery clouds; the great curved bench in the choir produces a shadow against which the pure light of the altar table, the splendour of candlesticks and chalice and the bright robes of the Pope and his assistants stand out the more clearly. On the left the spring-like colouring smiles, as it were, in the tender group of women. On the right the vivid outlines of the Swiss Guards are like intarsia in the surrounding colours. The Guards are crystalline and formal and static, which may be a tribute to Piero della Francesca, who had left some frescoes in this very room, which Raphael had to erase.

Was there perhaps a nocturnal scene among them — like the *Dream of Constantine* in Piero's frescoes in St Francesco in Assisi — such as might have inspired Raphael's very nocturnal *Liberation of St Peter?* (pag. 100 and PL. 37). The opposition of this lunette with its back to the light, owing to the window in the wall, was a situation deliberately chosen by Piero in his *Dream of Constantine* as being most suitable for his purposes, and the coincidence supports our theory, even if it remains a mere theory. Raphael here also over-comes every obstacle presented by the existence of the window, which he uses as part of the prison, by repeating its arch and its ironwork a second time. Certainly the scene is one of high imagination and great skill in execution.

The saint is asleep in chains in the prison. The angel appears in a halo of incandescent light 'which creates bright ice-like mirrors of light on the armour of the two soldiers asleep against the walls. They freeze like automata in that rush of light, their movements rigid like coleoptera ' (Ortolani). Has ever the image of the icy silence which surrounds a sleeper been so potently created, the 'automatisa-tion' of the human figure abandoned in sleep? On the right the angel leads St Peter by the hand towards freedom, while 'the helmets and cuirasses [of two other sleeping soldiers] struck by the rays of the angel, liquefy into a silver sheen: an achievement which will be repeated later by Caravaggio ' [in this Raphael anticipates Cara-vaggio's genius].

I do not see why Ortolani found the left-hand scene of the first alarm 'a somewhat tired conception of the spectacle'. For the digres-sion of episodes here, the brief insertion of minor figures belongs not only to Verdi and to Shakespeare, but forms the natural pause which is required to render the heroic action and the sublime event human. Vasari, who gave an excellent description of this fresco, writes of the ' sonorous ' effect of the scene on the left of the great grille: ' How great the terror and fright of those other armed guards outside the prison, when they hear the noise of the iron door, as a sentry with a torch wakes them, making a wisp of light which is echoed in every weapon, and where it does not reach, the light of the moon reaches'. St Peter coming out of the prison 'has the look on his face of it all being a dream, rather than reality ' and, of course, he did dream he would be freed, and in the morning, found himself outside the prison. Vasari also notes the wisdom of painting the scene against the light and draws attention to the same character in Piero della Francesca's composition. We agree with Vasari's conclusion ' for a thing which counterfeited night more closely than has ever been done in painting, this is the most divine, and held by all to be the most exceptional '.

With the *Isaiah* (circa 1512) in S. Agostino, frescoed under the influence of Michelangelo's Sistine ceiling, and the restless *Sybils* in Santa Maria della Pace (circa 1514) painted for Agostino Chigi, Raphael's work in the city ends.

After working in the Stanza of Heliodorus, Raphael was no longer capable of such divine flights of imagination and, for the most part, he entrusted the carrying out of his plans to his assistants. In the Stanza of the *Fire in the environs of St Peter's* (1514-17) there are four events commemorating Popes of the name of Leo, in honour of the reigning Pope Leo X. The fresco of the *Fire* itself shows signs of archaeological compromise where the figure of Aeneas fleeing from burning Troy is shown with two buildings whose columns are copied from existing Roman buildings, while the old façade of St Peter's soon to disappear, is also shown. This fresco has details of great beauty like Aeneas and Anchisis; the nude figure scrambling down the wall like a Marsyas held from on high, but unhurt and moving, seen in profile and with a view of his back; or the famous water-carrier with

PLATE 41 - PORTRAIT OF THE ' VELATA ' (C. 1513-1516) - FLORENCE, PITTI GALLERY

PLATE 42 - SISTINE MADONNA (C. 1514-1516) - DRESDEN, GALLERY

PLATE 43 - LEO X WITH TWO CARDINALS (C. 1518) - FLORENCE, PITTI GALLERY

PLATE 44 - TRANSFIGURATION (1518-1520) - VATICAN, GALLERY

the amphora on the right. But on the whole, archaeology takes the place of history, statuary replaces humanity and skill triumphs at the expense of poetry. The hand of Giulio Romano, of Penni or of Giovanni da Udine are more in evidence than the brush of Raphael.

Finally in the Hall of Constantine, the last of the halls for which Raphael was commissioned in 1517, the work was done after his death in 1524, under Clement VII, mainly by Giulio Romano and by Penni. These frescoes ' illustrate the defeat of paganism and the establishment of the Church of Rome. They mark the conclusion of the historical and political plan originally proposed by the Pope who ordered the frescoes' (Camesasca). Possibly the Master still observed the execution by Giulio Romano of his design for the *Battle of Ponte Milvio*, the gigantic prebaroque scene which became the pattern for all such scenes during the sixteenth century.

Other works executed by Giulio Romano, Penni, Raffaelino del Colle, Pierin del Vaga and Giovanni da Udine are of considerable interest on account of the decorative manner and language which derive from Raphael. Cardinal Bibbiena's bathroom (1516) in the Vatican is painted with grottesques and ornamental panels, quite classical in taste, inspired by Nero's Golden House which had just then been discovered. The subjects are somewhat profane — Venus, cupids etc — especially for a prelate. The loggia of *Psyche* in the Farnesina (1517), painted for Chigi, has a ceiling covered in a pergola so that the greenery in the garden on which the loggia looks out, is ideally continued indoors. The tales of Cupid and Psyche in the wings and in the tapestry-like ceiling and the figures of the cupids each with the symbols of victory over some divinity, are very academic but sensual, warm, amusing, brilliant, almost ironic, and tone in well with the pergola effect produced by Giovanni da Udine. The fount and the inspiration of Mannerism, which was beginning just then among painters like Beccafumi, lay in the so-called Bible of Raphael. There, a series of fifty-two illustrations of Old and New Testament stories painted in 1519 in the Vatican Loggias, surrounded by extremely rich decorative stuccos and grotesques, had combined mere illustration with clever classical mannerisms.

Then there are the ten tapestries intended for the Sistine Chapel, now in the Vatican Galleries, which were woven by Pieter van Aelst in Brussels after the cartoons by Raphael (1516-17) now at the Victoria and Albert Museum in London. They too have an almost audible classical eloquence, a prelude to Mannerism. Some of them, like the *Miracle of the haul of fish* or *the Conversion of St Paul* are also highly decorative.

Raphael imposes himself much more directly in easel paintings and they are a field for further experiment. We have already spoken of his portraits of high dignitaries of the Curia, of literary men, of financiers, of his beloved *Fornarina*, each of which excels in its kind. There are too paintings of a sacred nature, such as the custom of the age demanded.

A clear example of Raphael's school in the Bologna region was a Saint Cecilia (circa 1514), a painting which enjoyed great fame and had much influence. Four saints surround her central figure: at her feet is a still life of musical instruments by Giovanni da Udine. The *Madonna of the Fish* in the Prado, formerly in Naples, has a serene disposition of graceful forms, likewise the *Madonna dell'Impannata* in the Pitti, largely painted by assistants. The *Madonna della Seggiola* in the same gallery (PL. 40) is full of warmth and humanity.

This most popular of all paintings, unceasingly reproduced, could seem oleographic, but is in truth a masterpiece of Raphael. In her he idealized a very human image of the Madonna from a handsome and quite simple Roman woman, her head covered with a many-coloured shawl and her buxom child in her lap, with another child nearby. The vital warmth stems from the increasing intensity of the colouring as it comes out of the dark background, so that the warm contact between those two bodies clasped in the most elemental and natural affection is rendered in tones of colour. The figures are admirably suited to a round painting, and the roundness is echoed in the oval faces, in the rhythmic curve of the limbs, in the bent head of the little St John and in the segment of a circle which the restless feet of the Christ child occupy. Yet the natural truth of the figures is elevated, without any effort, by the moderation of his idealistic style. This is a classic which might be called both Christian and Catholic, in that it gathers together a given human situation, nature, the race, the social status, and transfigures all idealistically into a systematic and organic vision of the world that is optimistic, and does so with ' an universal feeling of affectionate tranquillity '.

The *Sistine Madonna* (PL. 42) — a rare painting on canvas of about 1516, made for the church of St Sisto in Piacenza and now in Dresden — is similarly naturalistic but ennobled by a clear and theatrically successful presentation of the image, such as would please the taste of the seventeenth century. The *Spasimo* (1517) in the Prado, the *St Michael* (1518) in the Louvre and the *Sainte Famille de François Ier* (1518), all painted for Leo X to give as presents to Francis Ist; the *Perla* and the *Holy Family under on Oak Tree* in the Prado and the *Visitation* there (signed, but executed by assistants) all have ' pre-mannerist accents [and an] exasperating colour and spatial sensuousness ' (Camesasca). The *Vision of Ezekiel* in which Vasari saw God painted ' in the manner of Jove ' does at least show the lion's claw, in ' lifting the viewer's eye to the celestial group, while the main actor in the miracle is relegated low down to the distance ' (Camesasca), a hitherto unheard of composition. Ezekiel does in fact appear minuscule, lit by a ray of light, in the landscape below.

The last and greatest masterpiece of Raphael was perhaps the *Leo X with Cardinals Giulio de' Medici and Luigi de' Rossi*, now in the Uffizi (PL. 43) which can be dated about 1519. The still life in this painting of the illuminated book and the precious bell on the table covered with red velvet, is superb, and, together with the full formalism of the figure and triumphant intonation of the various reds, serves to confirm the humanistic and hedonistic personality and the high dignity of the Medici Pope. There is even virtuosity in the back of the chair, and ' in the bronze gold ball which reflects like a mirror the light from the windows, the Pope's shoulders and the area of the room, so great is the clarity ' (Vasari).

A more debatable masterpiece is the *Transfiguration* (PL. 44) in the Vatican, begun by Raphael in 1518 most assiduously, to meet the ever-increasing criticisms about the way he handed much of his work to assistants, and also painted in competition with Sebastiano del Piombo's *Resurrection of Lazarus*. The upper part, composed in a marvellous semicircular area, is certainly sublime and carried out with a luminosity in the atmosphere that is worthy of a Venetian. Forms and colours are truly transfigured without losing their sculptural consistency. But in the lower part, the boy possessed who was, according to Matthew, brought to the disciples while they were assisting at the transfiguration of Christ, becomes theatrical and declamatory, and the luminosity is loud in light and shadow. The work was in fact unfinished when Raphael died on April 6, 1520, after a brief illness. It stood beside his deathbed and was later finished by Giulio Romano and Penni.

Vasari maintains that Raphael died of amorous excesses, but Müntz notes that ' if an excess of any kind caused the young Master's death, it would be overwork '. The immediate cause was probably one of those pernicious fevers which were frequent in Rome at the time. Marcantonio Michiel in a letter gave the evidence that ' the Pope himself was immeasurably grieved and during the fortnight of Raphael's illness sent him no less than six *fiats* (prayers for health). Imagine what others did... They say he has left 16,000 ducats, of which 5,000 in cash, most of which are to be distributed to his friends and servants [and, I imagine, to the Fornarina] and he has left his house which belonged to Bramante and which he purchased for 3,000 ducats to the Cardinal of Santa Maria in Portico [Bibbiena]. And he has been buried in the Rotonda where he was carried with honours. His soul will doubtless contemplate those heavenly buildings which never fade, but the memory of him and his name will stay here on earth in his works and in the minds of good men for a long time. There was much less harm, in my view, even if the plebs think differently, in the death of M. Agostino Gisi (Chigi) '.

Many others wept at the death of this great man. Some saw a divine premonition in a crack which opened just then in a wall of the Papal palace. Bembo's epitaph on the tomb of Raphael in the Pantheon in Rome ends with the familiar if rhetorical

'ILLE, HIC. EST RAPHAEL. TIMVIT. QUO. SOSPITE. VINCI
RERUM. MAGNA, PARENS. ET. MORIENTE. MORI'

and records the fact that the Master lived exactly 37 years, having died on his birthday.

This too is a coincidence, but it seems to symbolize, in the length of his life, a completed perfection like that of a circle or sphere, such as was the ideal principle and the fundamental basis of Raphael's art.

LIST OF ILLUSTRATIONS

LIST OF THE PLATES

LIST OF DRAWINGS